The Courage to Be You

Breaking Free from Fear and Embracing a Life You Love

Chrissy Shaver

Fitness Publishing

The Courage To Be You - Breaking Free from Fear and Embracing a Life You Love

Published by Fitness Marketing Group, Sunrise Beach, MO.

Printed in the United States of America

ISBN: 9798307935026

This publication is designed to provide accurate and authoritative information with regard to the subject matter covered. It is sold with the understanding that the publisher is not engaged in rendering legal, accounting, or other professional advice. If legal advice or other expert assistance is required, the services of a competent professional should be sought.

First edition

For more information, contact:

Positively Fitt, LLC 17431 N 71st Dr., suite 104 Glendale, AZ 85308

(623) 363-3792

Visit us online at: **https://positivelyfitt.com**

Table of Contents

Preface	V
Introduction	1
1. Why We Feel Invisible	7
2. The Weight of Guilt and Fear	18
3. Daydreams and Discontent	31
4. The Power of Self-Awareness	43
5. Your Voice Matters	56
6. Silencing the Inner Critic	69
7. Prioritizing You Without Guilt	82
8. Setting Boundaries That Stick	94
9. Taking Inspired Action	106
10. Leading with Your Heart	119
11. Conclusion	133
12. Epilogue	139

13. Your Next Step... 143

About the Author 146

Preface

***"The only limit to our realization of tomorrow will be our doubts of today."* — Franklin D. Roosevelt**

This quote elegantly underscores the essence of this book: confronting and overcoming the self-doubt that often shackles us to complacency. *The Courage to Be You* explores the intricate dance between fulfilling daily responsibilities and nurturing your own well-being. It's about breaking free from the fears that cloud your true potential and embracing a life brimming with authenticity and joy.

Writing this book was driven by a deep understanding of the struggles faced by many women who juggle numerous roles—caregivers, professionals, partners, parents—often sidelining their own dreams and desires in the process. The aim here is clear: to offer you, the reader, a blueprint for rediscovering your own needs and desires without feeling guilty for prioritizing them.

I've been fortunate to connect with numerous women who shared their journeys of self-neglect due to overwhelming daily demands. One such story that deeply resonated with me was of Anna, a dedicated nurse and mother of three, who confessed during a workshop that she couldn't remember the last time she did something just for herself. Her story is not unique, but is a powerful reminder of why this book is necessary. These narratives fueled my commitment to provide a resource that could truly make a difference.

The insights in these pages are backed by research, discussions with psychologists, and countless conversations with women who are living proof of the book's strategies. Their transformations from overwhelmed and self-doubting to confident and engaged in their own lives provided the real-world validation that these methods work.

I am immensely grateful to all who have contributed to this journey—the mentors, peers, family members, and especially the brave women who shared their stories. Their experiences and insights have been invaluable.

To everyone who has picked up this book, thank you for investing your time and trust in these pages. I write not only to share knowledge but to ignite a conversation about how we can realistically care for ourselves amidst our busy lives.

This book is tailored for women aged 25 to 65, who find themselves perpetually balancing the needs of others against their own, often at the cost of their personal well-being. No prior knowledge is necessary, just an open mind and the willingness to engage with the material sincerely.

As you turn these pages, I invite you to embrace the ideas laid out before you, apply the practical advice, and visualize a life where you stand confident and fulfilled. Thank you for choosing to take this step. I look forward to hearing how your life unfolds as you apply the wisdom found here.

Introduction

The Cost of Neglecting Yourself

If you've ever felt invisible in your own life, you're not alone. Maybe you've stood in a room full of people, smiling and nodding, while silently wondering if anyone truly saw you. Or maybe you've spent years focusing on everyone else—your kids, your partner, your career—until there wasn't a single ounce of energy left for yourself. Somewhere along the way, you stopped being the main character in your own story and became the supporting cast for everyone else's.

This book is here to tell you something important: ***that ends now.***

The truth is, life didn't come with a manual for how to juggle everything and still feel whole. Society teaches women to be caretakers first and people second. It applauds you for running yourself ragged, sacrificing your needs, and putting yourself last. But where does that leave you? Exhausted, unfulfilled, and wondering why it feels like something's missing.

Maybe you've ignored that feeling for years, brushing it aside because you've convinced yourself that taking care of yourself is selfish. But here's the thing: self-care isn't selfish. It's survival. You can't pour from an empty cup, and you certainly can't show up as the best version of yourself when you're running on fumes.

This isn't about abandoning your responsibilities or the people you love. It's about understanding that you deserve a seat at the table of your own life. It's about remembering that your needs, your dreams, and your desires matter. It's about reclaiming the parts of yourself that you've tucked away for too long.

Who This Book Is For

This book is for women like you. Women who've spent years prioritizing everyone else and have reached a point where they feel stuck, unseen, and unsure of who they are anymore. It's for the women who wake up each day with a nagging sense of discontent, wondering, *"Is this all there is?"* and *"When do I get to matter?"*

You might be that woman who always feels like the underdog—like no matter how hard you try, you're not quite enough. Maybe you're the woman who daydreams about what life could look like if you weren't afraid to take the leap, but you're too scared of being judged or failing. Maybe you've buried those dreams so deep, you've forgotten what they even look like.

Does this sound familiar? You're constantly busy, constantly needed, but never truly fulfilled. You're amazing at showing up for everyone else but struggle to show up for yourself. You tell yourself, *"I'll focus on me someday, when things calm down,"* but that *"someday"* never comes.

Here's the thing: this book isn't going to guilt you or shame you into action. That's not what you need. What you need is someone who understands where you are right now—someone who can help you take the first small, manageable steps toward a life that feels meaningful and true to you.

This book is that guide.

What's Possible for You

Let me paint you a picture of what's possible: Imagine waking up in the morning and feeling excited about the day ahead. Imagine looking in the mirror and seeing a woman who's confident, radiant, and unapologetically herself. Imagine having the energy to pursue your dreams, the courage to speak your mind, and the peace of knowing you've finally made space for yourself in your own life.

That's not just a fantasy—it's within your reach.

When you finish this book, you'll have the tools to make that vision a reality. You'll learn how to break free from the fears and doubts that have been holding you back. You'll discover how to create boundaries that protect your time and energy without feeling guilty. You'll explore practical ways to reconnect with your passions, build confidence, and take action toward the life you've always wanted.

This isn't about *"fixing"* you, because you're not broken. It's about uncovering the version of you that's been buried under years of self-doubt, guilt, and societal expectations. It's about helping you see yourself the way the people who love you sec you—as someone worthy of happiness, success, and love.

Every chapter in this book is designed to guide you, step by step, toward a life where you no longer feel like the underdog. You'll laugh, you might cry, and you'll definitely have a few *"aha"* moments along the way. Most importantly, you'll come away from this journey feeling empowered (in your own way) to take back your life, one intentional step at a time.

Are You Ready?

You're here because you know there's more waiting for you. You've felt the nudge, the whisper in your heart telling you that you're capable of so much more than just surviving. You're ready to stop hiding, stop playing small, and start showing up for yourself in ways you never have before.

I won't promise this will be easy, but I can promise it will be worth it. The courage to be you has always been inside of you—it's just been waiting for the right moment to rise.

That moment is now. Let's get started.

Chapter One

Why We Feel Invisible

Can Taking Time for Oneself Truly Benefit Others?

Mara walked through the brisk morning, her breath visible in the cold air, a rhythmic puff that matched her steady pace. The park was quiet, except for the rustling of leaves and the distant bark of a dog. She was usually surrounded by the chaos of her family's needs—her children's school projects, her partner's work schedules—but today she walked alone.

She thought about the argument she had with her sister last night. *"You always take on too much,"* her sister had said, frustration lining her voice. *"When do you ever take time for yourself?"* Mara had brushed off the concern with a shrug, insisting she was fine, but as she walked, she couldn't shake off a creeping sense of exhaustion that seemed to weigh down each step.

The park bench looked inviting against the backdrop of golden leaves and Mara sat down, letting out a sigh. She watched a mother playing with her child nearby, their laughter floating across to where Mara sat wrapped in her own contemplations. It dawned on her how rarely she allowed herself moments like these—simple, quiet moments where no demands were made of her.

Her phone buzzed in her pocket—a reminder of a PTA meeting she had promised to attend. Mara silenced it momentarily and closed her eyes. The sounds of the park filled her ears; children's laughter mingled with the whispering trees and chirping birds. She realized how disconnected she felt from these sounds usually, always preoccupied with tasks and responsibilities.

Opening her eyes again, Mara felt a resolve forming within her. Maybe there was truth in what her sister said. If she were more rested, more at peace with herself, perhaps she could offer more to those around her—not just fulfilling obligations but being truly present for them.

As Mara stood up from the bench and started back towards home, a question lingered in her mind: If we all took a little more time for ourselves, could we change not just our lives but also enrich those around us?

Are You Really Putting Yourself First?

In a world where the demands of daily life seem to leave little room for personal reflection, it's no wonder many feel like they've lost touch with themselves. The first chapter of this pivotal guide addresses the crucial, often overlooked aspect of self-care and its broader implications not just for individuals, but for the communities they are part of. It challenges the deep-seated belief that taking care of oneself is a selfish act, instead proposing that true community care begins with individual well-being.

Self-care is more than just an occasional spa day—it's a vital component in the machinery of communal health and vitality. When we neglect our own needs, we are less able to contribute effectively to our families and communities. This chapter sets the stage by debunking myths about self-care, highlighting its role as a cornerstone for building stronger, more resilient community bonds.

Identifying What Holds Us Back

The feeling of invisibility doesn't manifest overnight; it evolves from ingrained habits and societal narratives that consistently place others' needs before our own. Recognizing these patterns is the first step toward breaking free. This chapter will guide you through understanding these invisible threads that weave through your daily routines, subtly sewing seeds of neglect toward your own needs.

The Weight of Expectations

Unrealistic standards and a culture of over-giving often skew our perception of what it means to be successful and content. Here, we'll explore how these expectations have shaped your sense of self-worth and discuss strategies to recalibrate your understanding of what it really means to lead a fulfilling life.

A New Beginning

Acknowledging the need for change is one thing; taking the first step is another. This chapter doesn't just highlight the problem—it offers practical, actionable solutions.

Small but significant shifts in mindset can illuminate your path forward, helping you reclaim your visibility in your own life and in your community.

Throughout this book, you'll find that each strategy and insight is designed not only to help you reconnect with yourself but also to prepare you to give back to those around you more effectively. By fostering a better understanding of not just self-care, but BADASS self-care or not just self-care but reclaiming your hearts BADASSERY while rediscovering self-care, we lay down the foundation for stronger interpersonal relationships and healthier communities.

This exploration isn't just about overcoming fear or breaking free from old habits; it's about constructing a life where balance, happiness, and health are within your reach. Remember: when you thrive, so does your community.

Real-life success stories interspersed throughout this text will show you that these strategies are not only theoretical but also practical and achievable. These narratives underscore the profound impact that prioritizing self-care can have on both personal growth and community well-being.

As we navigate through this chapter and those that follow, keep in mind that this is not just about personal transformation—it's about cultivating an environment where everyone can thrive. By caring for ourselves, we are setting a powerful example for others and enhancing our ability to contribute positively to our world.

Recognizing Invisible Patterns

At the core of feeling overlooked lies a series of invisible patterns and habits that we seldom question. These patterns are often woven into our daily lives through societal expectations and cultural narratives. By recognizing these, individuals can begin to understand how these influences contribute to a sense of invisibility.

Imagine your daily routines and interactions as threads in a vast net. Some of these threads are so thin and blended into the background that you barely notice them. However, they significantly shape your perception of self and your interactions with others. Identifying these threads—these patterns—is the first step towards visibility.

Societal narratives particularly impact women, who are frequently taught to prioritize the needs of others above their own. This can manifest in always saying yes to requests, putting family and work obligations before personal health, and rarely allocating time for self-care. Over time, this pattern of behavior can lead to a diminishing sense of self-worth and identity.

Exploring these habitual responses requires honest self-reflection. It involves questioning why we act in certain ways and whether these actions serve our well-being or simply comply with external expectations. This process isn't about assigning blame, but about gaining clarity and understanding the roots of our actions.

Recognizing these patterns is crucial for breaking the cycle of invisibility.

Understanding the Role of Expectations

Expectations can be hefty burdens. Often, they are like invisible weights we carry, molded by societal standards and personal ambitions. For many, particularly women, these expectations involve a high degree of self-sacrifice and over-giving, which can erode one's sense of self over time.

Have you ever considered how much of your day is spent meeting others' expectations? From perfection at work to an immaculate home or even the unspoken rules of social engagement, the standards set for us and by us can be unreasonably high. This relentless pursuit can lead to exhaustion and a feeling of invisibility, as if one's true Self is buried under the weight of trying to measure up.

Using an analogy, think of each expectation as a brick in a backpack you carry. Each brick represents a demand or a standard you feel compelled to meet. As more bricks are added, the heavier the backpack gets, until the weight is so overwhelming that it's impossible to move freely. Understanding this can be a revelation in recognizing how much we impose upon ourselves.

Questioning these expectations is not about seeking excuses but about re-evaluating what truly matters. It's about distinguishing between what enriches our lives and what depletes us. This distinction is vital for mental health and for cultivating a life that feels genuinely fulfilling rather than one that merely looks good from the outside.

Are the expectations you carry serving you, or are they diminishing your light?

The First Step Toward Visibility

The journey toward feeling seen and valued begins with small, yet significant, shifts in mindset. Acknowledging that you deserve to prioritize your well-being is a revolutionary act of self-recognition. This acknowledgment is the first step toward reclaiming your visibility.

Consider how a small shift in thinking can change everything. For example, deciding to spend the first 30 minutes of your day engaged in a personal activity you enjoy, whether reading, yoga, or simply sitting quietly with a cup of coffee, can set a positive tone for the day. This act, though small, reinforces the notion that your needs matter.

Integrating such small changes consistently can lead to significant transformations over time. It's like planting a seed. Initially, it's just a small object buried in soil, but with consistent care and nurturing, it grows into a strong, visible plant. Similarly, small acts of self-care and self-recognition can grow into a robust sense of some BadAssery, where your Self refuses to be invisible.

By prioritizing self-care, you enhance your ability to care for others, creating a healthier community around you. This realization links all our learning

objectives, emphasizing the profound impact of nurturing oneself on individual and communal levels.

As we wrap up this initial exploration into why feelings of invisibility persist, it's crucial to recognize that the path to visibility begins with **self-awareness and self-care**. By identifying invisible patterns and understanding the burdens of unrealistic expectations, you have taken essential steps toward reclaiming your identity. These insights are not just about personal growth; they play a critical role in how you interact with and contribute to your community.

Self-care is foundational, not selfish. It equips you to offer more genuine support to those around you, enhancing the well-being of both yourself and your community. This shift from feeling invisible to becoming an active, visible participant in your own life encourages a healthier, more balanced approach to both personal ambitions and communal responsibilities.

As you move forward, remember that small mindset shifts can create significant life changes. The strategies discussed here are just the beginning. With each chapter, you will discover more about yourself and the immense value you bring to every space you enter. The upcoming chapters promise even more insights and practical advice to help you live authentically and with confidence.

Get ready to explore deeper, challenge old beliefs, and build a life filled with purpose and presence. The benefits awaiting you are profound and transformative, offering not only personal fulfillment but also a stronger connection with those around you. Your courage to face these challenges head-on will inspire and uplift, creating ripples of positive change that extend far beyond your immediate surroundings.

Chapter Two

The Weight of Guilt and Fear

Can Patience Truly Shape Our Destiny?

Elena stood by the window, watching the slow dance of autumn leaves as they twirled gracefully to the ground. The crisp air brushed against her face, carrying whispers of change. Inside her small, cluttered apartment, the walls seemed to close in with every tick of the clock. She thought about her recent promotion at work—an event she had yearned for over years of meticulous effort and quiet perseverance.

Her mind wandered back to the countless evenings spent refining project proposals, each line a testament to her unwavering commitment. Yet now, as the reality of her new role settled in, doubts crept into her heart like uninvited shadows at dusk. Was she truly ready? Could she meet the lofty expectations set before her?

As she mulled over these thoughts, a neighbor's laughter floated up from the street below, slicing through her reverie. It reminded Elena of simpler times when success was measured by small, personal victories—learning a new recipe, finishing a challenging book, helping a friend in need.

The soft chime of her phone broke the silence again. It was a message from an old mentor: *"Remember, growth is not instant. It's all about patience and consistency."* These words echoed in Elena's mind as she considered her journey thus far. Each step had been small but significant—none were without struggle or doubt.

She poured herself a glass of water, its coolness refreshing against her lips and grounding her thoughts. The kitchen sink leaked slightly; each drop echoed like a metronome counting down moments of uncertainty. She tightened the faucet with more resolve than necessary—a small victory over household decay.

As night drew its dark curtain across the city skyline, Elena sat down with an old notebook filled with goals and reflections from years past. Flipping through it was like walking down a memory lane paved with both triumphs and setbacks—all leading to this very moment.

In this quiet hour of introspection, how might we all see our paths differently if we viewed each challenge as a necessary stitch in the fabric of our growth?

Are You Ready to Challenge the Myths of Instant Transformation?

In an age dominated by instant gratification and quick fixes, we often find ourselves caught up in the allure of immediate results, especially when it comes to personal growth. **"The Courage to Be You: Breaking Free from Fear and Embracing a Life You Love"** introduces a compelling counter-narrative in its second chapter, emphasizing that real change is not instantaneous but a slow and steady process. This chapter lays the groundwork for understanding how embracing a gradual approach to self-improvement can profoundly impact our lives.

The Slow Road to Self-Improvement

It's crucial to start by debunking a common myth: the idea that personal transformation must be swift to be effective. This misconception can lead to frustration and a sense of inadequacy when the results aren't immediate. The truth is, sustainable growth requires patience, perseverance, and a series of small, consistent steps. By setting realistic expectations, we allow ourselves the space and time necessary for true development.

Facing Guilt Head-On

One of the significant barriers many face in prioritizing personal growth is guilt. Often, taking time for ourselves feels like a luxury at the expense of others. This chapter will explore why this guilt forms and how letting go of it is not just beneficial but essential for our well-being. Understanding the roots of this guilt helps dismantle it, clearing the path toward prioritizing our development without the weight of undue self-reproach.

Permission to Start Small

Often overlooked is the power of beginning with manageable steps. The notion that every action towards personal improvement must be groundbreaking adds unnecessary pressure. This chapter encourages starting small—highlighting how incremental changes can build up to significant transformations over time. It reassures readers that modest beginnings are not only acceptable but often more effective.

Each section of this chapter uses practical examples and actionable advice to bring these ideas to life, making them relatable and achievable. By addressing these critical barriers—guilt, fear of judgment, and the pressure for grand gestures—the chapter equips readers with the tools needed for authentic self-improvement.

As we move forward, remember: patience isn't just a virtue; it's a necessity for change. Acknowledging this can free us from the chains of immediacy and open us up to a world where growth is both a process and a reward in itself. With each small step, we move closer to becoming who we truly aspire to be—free from fear and full of life.

This insightful approach not only sets a realistic pace for personal development but also aligns perfectly with the overall theme of the book—encouraging readers to live authentically despite life's challenges. By turning these pages, you are not just reading; you are stepping into a mindset that celebrates every small victory on the path to greater self-realization.

Facing Guilt Head-On

Guilt often accompanies the decision to prioritize oneself, rooted deeply in societal and cultural expectations. It's that unpleasant feeling that arises when you choose your own needs over others', whether it's taking time for self-care, pursuing personal goals, or simply saying no to additional responsibilities. Understanding where this guilt comes from is the first step towards overcoming it.

Imagine guilt as a heavy backpack you carry around. Each time you put yourself first, another rock of *'should-have'* or *'could-have'* is added. Over time, this load can become unbearable, unless you consciously decide to unpack these rocks and examine them. Are they really yours to carry? More often than not, they are expectations and norms imposed by society, not personal truths.

The importance of letting go of guilt cannot be understated. By shedding these burdens, you empower yourself to make decisions that truly benefit your well-being without the extra weight of undue guilt. This shift in perspective is essential for personal growth and happiness.

Letting go begins with recognizing that caring for yourself is not an act of selfishness but of necessity. Each act of self-priority is a step towards a healthier, more balanced life. It's about giving yourself the permission to thrive without the shadow of guilt.

Understanding and releasing guilt is crucial for personal development.

Unpacking Fear of Judgment

Another obstacle that frequently impedes progress is the fear of judgment. Worrying about others' opinions can keep us from taking even the smallest step forward. This section will examine how societal expectations can lead to self-censorship and stagnation. It will also provide strategies for overcoming these fears, reinforcing the idea that our personal growth journey should be dictated by our values and goals, not those imposed by others.

The fear of judgment can be paralyzing. It keeps many from expressing their true selves or pursuing their dreams, tethered by the potential criticism of others. This fear is often ingrained from a young age, reinforced by experiences and societal messages that value conformity over individuality.

Criticism, real or imagined, can have a profound effect on our decisions. It shapes behavior and often leads to playing it safe rather than risking disapproval. This not only stifles creativity, but also prevents personal growth. The first step in overcoming this fear is recognizing its presence and understanding its roots.

Consider the analogy of walking on a tightrope. The fear of falling (judgment) can be so overwhelming that it distracts from the ability to balance and move forward. However, by focusing on each step and trusting your ability to reach the other side, you effectively reduce the impact of fear.

Creating a mental shift involves questioning the power you give to others' opinions. Why should someone else's judgment define your worth or dictate your actions? This realization can be liberating and is the first step towards reclaiming your life from the shadows of fear.

What would you attempt if you knew you could not fail?

Permission to Start Small

Starting small is often underestimated in a world that celebrates big leaps and instant results. However, small, intentional actions are foundational to sustainable growth. They allow you to build confidence, gather feedback, and adjust your course without the overwhelming pressure of massive expectations.

Think of it as planting a garden. Each seed represents a small action; watering it daily demonstrates the consistency needed for growth. Over time, these small seeds grow into a flourishing garden, a direct result of daily, consistent care.

Small steps accumulate into significant progress. They make the process manageable and less daunting, increasing the likelihood of persistence and success. This approach is not only practical but also psychologically beneficial. It builds momentum and reinforces the belief in one's ability to achieve goals.

By embracing the philosophy of starting small, you give yourself the chance to experiment and learn without the paralyzing fear of large-scale failure. Each small step forward is a victory in itself, reinforcing your confidence and gradually leading to larger achievements.

Facing guilt, overcoming fear, and starting small are interconnected steps towards personal growth. Each element supports the other, creating a robust framework for sustainable self-improvement and a fulfilling life.

The insights we've explored in this chapter underscore the pivotal role of gradual growth in personal development. By facing guilt head-on, unpacking the fear of judgment, and granting ourselves permission to start small, we set the stage for sustained progress. Each of these strategies is not just about making changes, but about understanding the deeper reasons behind our feelings and behaviors, which is essential for true transformation.

Step-by-Step Guide: Navigating Guilt and Embracing Self-Prioritization

Objective: To effectively manage and overcome guilt associated with prioritizing oneself, leading to improved well-being and personal fulfillment.

1. Acknowledge and Record: Begin by recognizing your feelings of guilt. Write down instances where you've prioritized others at your expense and note the emotions tied to these moments.

- *Timeframe: 1 week*

2. Analyze the Causes: Reflect on why these feelings emerge. Is it due to societal pressures, personal expectations, or fear of letting others down? Understanding these triggers is crucial.

- *Timeframe: 1-2 days*

3. List the Benefits of Letting Go: Write down how releasing guilt can enhance your life, such as improved mental health and more authentic relationships.

- *Timeframe: 1 day*

4. Practice Self-Compassion: Engage in self-compassion techniques like affirmations or positive self-talk. Remind yourself of your worth and right to prioritize your needs.

- *Timeframe: Ongoing*

5. Take Intentional Action: Choose an activity that focuses on your needs, like pursuing a hobby or practicing mindfulness. Notice how you feel afterwards and journal your thoughts.

- *Timeframe: 1 week*

6. Reflect and Adjust: Regularly assess how these actions affect your feelings of guilt. Adjust your approach as needed, aiming for a gradual reduction in guilt.

- *Timeframe: Ongoing*

7. Seek Feedback: Discuss your feelings and progress with someone you trust, like a friend or therapist. This can provide new insights and reinforce your efforts.

- *Timeframe: Ongoing*

This process is designed to be flexible, allowing you to tailor it to your unique circumstances while providing a clear framework for addressing and overcoming guilt.

By embracing these practical steps, you lay a foundation for not only combating guilt but also for fostering a life where personal growth and self-care are harmonized. This balance is crucial for anyone looking to lead a fulfilling life while effectively managing daily responsibilities and societal expectations.

Remember, the path to self-improvement is continuous and requires persistence and resilience. Each small step forward is a building block in constructing a more confident and contented Self. So, give yourself the grace to grow at your own pace, understanding that each phase of growth enriches your journey towards a more authentic life.

Chapter Three

Daydreams and Discontent

Can Confidence Be Cultivated Like a Garden?

In the soft glow of early morning, Joan stood by her window, looking out at the small patch of garden she had started last spring. The tomatoes were just beginning to ripen, a vivid red against the green. Her hands rested on the windowsill, fingers tapping lightly, mirroring the rhythm of his doubts. Today was the day she would present her project proposal to the board—an idea she had nurtured as carefully as her garden.

The room around her was quiet, save for the ticking of the old clock on the mantle. She could hear her own breathing, each inhale sharp and each exhale shaky. It was this moment before stepping into battle that always seemed to stretch endlessly. Her mind raced back to her mentor's words last week: *"Confidence isn't born, Joan; it's built."*

She recalled her early days in this very room when failure seemed more frequent than success. Each setback had been a storm, each triumph a sunny day. Now, as she mulled over her presentation, she felt those old, familiar seeds of doubt sprouting once again.

A sudden chirp from a bird outside drew her attention away from the dark spirals of her thoughts. She watched as it hopped along the branch of an oak tree—so fearless in its smallness. Joan smiled faintly; there was something profoundly inspiring about its simple existence.

As she turned from the window and grabbed her notes from the desk, a reflection caught in the mirror stopped her—a woman much older than she felt inside, yet with eyes that still held a spark of youthful determination. Today needed to be about more than just presenting an idea; it needed to be about proving to herself that all these years had built not just skill but also resilience and confidence.

She walked through the hallway lined with photographs—moments captured in time that spoke of both joy and struggle—and each step seemed to echo louder in her ears, as if urging her forward.

At breakfast, her husband handed her a cup of coffee with that knowing look in his eyes—the one that said he believed in her even when she struggled to believe in herself. The warmth from the mug seeped into her hands and with it came a subtle shift inside her—a gentle reminder that growth often comes quietly.

As Joan left for work with her briefcase in hand and determination setting into every line on her face, she wondered if today might be another milestone—the kind you look back on and realize it was bigger than you thought at the time.

Could it be true that every challenge faced is another opportunity to nurture our own garden of confidence?

Is Confidence Truly Built, Not Born?

Confidence is not a static trait; it's a dynamic state that evolves through deliberate practice and mindset shifts. This chapter unpacks the misconception that confidence is purely an inborn quality and instead proposes practical ways to foster and strengthen this crucial aspect of self-identity. By examining your internal dialogues and external actions, you can initiate significant personal growth.

Recognizing the Signals of Unfulfilled Potential

Every individual harbors dreams that often get sidelined by daily responsibilities and fears. These daydreams are not just whimsical thoughts but vital signs pointing towards your deeper desires and untapped potential. Acknowledging these signals is the first step toward understanding what truly motivates you and where your passions lie.

Turning Frustration into Purpose

It's common to feel stuck or frustrated when there's a gap between where you are and where you want to be. However, this frustration can be transformed into a valuable resource. By channeling these feelings into focused action, you can create a clear path forward, turning obstacles into stepping stones towards your goals.

Articulating Your Desires Clearly

Clarity is power. The ability to articulate your desires without fear or hesitation is crucial for progress. This section will provide you with tools to prioritize your goals and express them clearly, setting the stage for achievement. Clear communication of your aspirations is essential not just for personal clarity but also for enlisting the support of others in your journey.

Practical steps play a pivotal role in building confidence. Setting small, achievable goals can lead to quick wins, which in turn boost your sense of self-efficacy. Similarly, engaging in projects that ignite your passion can rekindle enthusiasm and reinforce your self-confidence.

Professional guidance, whether through mentoring, coaching, or structured programs, can also accelerate this process. These resources provide not only expert advice but also accountability that helps maintain momentum.

Moreover, the simple act of **writing down** goals and regularly reviewing them can significantly enhance your focus and drive. Visualization techniques further support this process by helping you mentally rehearse success scenarios, which prepares you psychologically to face challenges head-on.

In essence, confidence is like a muscle that strengthens with use. By understanding your desires, redirecting your frustrations into productive channels, and articulating your goals with precision, you set the foundation for robust self-esteem that propels you toward a life you love.

This chapter aims not just to inspire but to equip you with the knowledge and tools necessary for transforming passive daydreaming into active life-shaping strategy. As we explore these ideas together, remember that each step taken is a move towards becoming more authentically yourself—a person equipped with both the courage and clarity to live passionately and purposefully.

Understanding Your Longing

Daydreams are often dismissed as frivolous fantasies or idle thoughts. Yet, they hold a much deeper significance. They are the mind's way of signaling desires that go beyond our immediate reality, hinting at potential and aspirations yet to be explored. Recognizing these signals is the first step toward understanding what we truly long for in life.

Imagine your daydreams as light beams escaping through cracks in a darkened room. These beams illuminate what is outside our current experience, guiding us towards what we might yet achieve or become. This metaphor helps us see daydreams not as mere distractions, but as beacons pointing toward a fuller, more satisfying life.

It's not uncommon to feel a sense of discontent when comparing our current state to the ideals we daydream about. This feeling isn't just normal; it's a useful indicator that our current situation might not fully align with our deeper aspirations. Acknowledging this can be uncomfortable, but it's crucial for real growth.

Engaging with our daydreams can often reveal a pattern. Perhaps you consistently imagine yourself in a leadership role or envision a life filled with creative expression. These recurring themes are clues worth examining. They can reveal core aspects of our identity and ambition that demand more attention and development.

Daydreams are valuable signals that point to our unfulfilled potential and deepest desires.

From Frustration to Focus

Turning frustration into focus begins with understanding the root cause of our frustrations. Often, they stem from a disparity between where we are and where we want to be. Acknowledging this gap is the first step toward bridging it.

Frustration, though uncomfortable, is a powerful motivator. It pushes us to change and can catapult significant personal growth. By channeling this energy constructively, we transform our frustrations into a focused drive to achieve our goals.

Consider the frustration of a sculptor whose block of marble won't yet reveal the envisioned masterpiece. Each chip of the chisel directed by frustration can help clarify the vision, driving the sculptor to persist until the form hidden within is finally unveiled. This analogy illustrates how frustration can be a tool for refinement and clarity in our pursuits.

To effectively turn frustration into focus, it's essential to set clear, achievable goals. This process involves breaking down large aspirations into smaller, manageable tasks that can be tackled one at a time. This not only provides a clear path forward but also offers regular milestones to celebrate, maintaining motivation.

Strategies such as mindfulness and cognitive restructuring can also be invaluable. They help us manage our emotional responses and reshape our perspective towards challenges. Seeing obstacles as opportunities to learn and grow reduces feelings of frustration and enhances our focus and productivity.

Could reframing your frustrations as stepping stones to success change your perspective and increase your effectiveness?

Creating Clarity

Achieving clarity about our desires requires honest self-reflection. It's about identifying what we truly want, not what we think we should want based on societal expectations or other external pressures. This clarity is essential for setting goals that resonate with our true selves.

One effective method to enhance clarity is to create a vision board. This tool allows individuals to visually articulate their desires, making abstract aspirations concrete and tangible. By selecting images and words that resonate with their goals and aspirations, individuals can create a powerful visual reminder of their path forward.

Imagine your desires as a garden. Just as a gardener plans which plants to cultivate, you must decide which desires to nurture and which to weed out. This analogy helps illustrate the importance of prioritizing desires that truly align with your personal growth and fulfillment.

Regularly revisiting and revising our goals is crucial as we evolve and our circumstances change. This dynamic approach ensures that our objectives remain relevant and aligned with our deepest desires. It prevents us from pursuing outdated goals that no longer serve our best interests.

By understanding our daydreams, transforming our frustrations, and clarifying our desires, we craft a life that is not only successful but also deeply fulfilling.

As we wrap up our exploration into the significance of daydreams and discontent, it's essential to recognize that these elements are not just whimsical thoughts or mere frustrations. Rather, they are crucial indicators of your deeper desires and untapped potential. By understanding your longing, you can begin to see these daydreams as the first step toward a more fulfilling life.

Transforming frustration into focus is about harnessing the energy from your discontent and channeling it into a powerful drive for change. This shift is pivotal. It moves you from a state of passivity to one of active pursuit of your goals. This is where clarity plays a critical role. By creating clarity, you not only articulate what you truly want, but also outline the actionable steps needed to achieve these desires.

The process we've discussed is not just about making minor adjustments to your daily routine; it's about initiating a profound shift in how you view and interact with your world. This shift is necessary for building the kind of confidence that is not innate but developed through intentional action and a change in mindset. The strategies outlined—setting clear goals, engaging deeply with your passions, and seeking professional guidance—are practical and structured ways to enhance your self-esteem and foster personal growth.

By adopting these practices, you not only improve your ability to achieve what you desire but also strengthen your capacity to face new challenges. Confidence grows when you step out of your comfort zone and tackle obstacles head-on, using the tools you've gained.

Remember, each step you take in refining your focus and clarifying your goals contributes significantly to building a resilient, confident self. As you move forward, keep in mind that the clarity you develop today lays the groundwork for the achievements of tomorrow.

Take these insights and apply them consistently. Your dedication to understanding and reshaping your daydreams and frustrations into a clear, actionable plan will be the key driver of your success. It's about taking control of your narrative and making those crucial decisions that align with your deepest values and aspirations.

Let this chapter serve as a foundation upon which you build a more confident, focused, and fulfilled self. The path ahead is clear, and it leads to a life where your aspirations are not just daydreams but realities shaped by your own hands.

Chapter Four

The Power of Self-Awareness

Can Small Acts of Self-Care Shift the Weight of the World?

Amelia sat at the edge of her garden, her hands buried in the rich, dark soil. The sun was high and relentless, but under the broad leaves of an old oak tree, she found a sliver of shade that cooled her flushed cheeks. The garden was small, a humble array of herbs and a few hardy flowers that fought bravely through the cracks in the pavement. It was her sanctuary from the endless demands of life—a demanding job, a bustling household, and a constant battle with exhaustion.

As she plucked a wilting daisy from its stem, she mused over her recent struggles with anxiety. The weight seemed tangible some days, pressing down on her chest until it was hard to breathe. She had read somewhere that small acts of self-care could help alleviate these overwhelming feelings. *"Could something as simple as sitting here, touching earth, mend the frayed edges of my mind?"* she wondered silently.

Her thoughts were interrupted by the laughter of children playing in the street; their carefree voices floated over the fences, mingling with the rustle of leaves and chirping birds. Amelia watched them for a moment, remembering how little it took to make them happy—a popsicle on a hot day or a game of tag under the sun. *"Maybe happiness is stitched together from small moments like these,"* she thought.

The idea settled in her like seeds in fertile soil; maybe she didn't need grand gestures to find peace. Perhaps what she needed were pockets of time: five minutes to drink tea on this very bench or ten minutes to walk barefoot across this grass.

As dusk approached and painted the sky in strokes of orange and purple, Amelia stood up slowly. Her body felt lighter somehow, as if acknowledging these tiny rituals had lifted part of the burden from her shoulders.

She walked back into her house with muddy boots and a quiet smile—tomorrow she would try again with another small act: maybe waking up ten minutes earlier to watch dawn break or reading just one page from that book collecting dust on her shelf.

Could it be that within these fleeting moments lies an untapped reservoir of calm?

Is Self-Care Truly Achievable Amidst Life's Chaos?

In a world that incessantly demands more—more hours, more energy, more perfection—it's no wonder that the notion of self-care can seem like a distant luxury rather than a feasible part of everyday life. Yet, it is precisely in these overwhelming times that self-care becomes not just beneficial but essential. For women navigating the relentless pressures of daily responsibilities, recognizing and integrating small, manageable acts of self-care can pave the way to substantial mental and emotional relief.

Self-awareness is your greatest ally. It allows you to see your life through a lens of where you can realistically incorporate these practices without feeling burdened by them. This chapter explores how small steps, like brief meditations or quick walks, are not only doable but can also cumulatively lead to profound impacts on your wellbeing.

Discovering Your Strengths

Before diving into what self-care strategies might work for you, it's crucial to first understand your strengths. Many women overlook their capabilities and undervalue their achievements because they compare themselves to an often unattainable societal standard. This section will guide you through simple exercises designed to help you identify and appreciate your unique skills, values, and passions. This isn't about transforming who you are; it's about reinforcing your confidence in what you already bring to the table.

Defining Personal Success

Our definition of success can sometimes feel like it's been scripted for us by society. However, true satisfaction comes from achieving what matters personally to us, not what is expected by others. In this part of the chapter, we'll look at how redefining success on your own terms can liberate you from unnecessary pressures and align your life with your genuine aspirations.

Aligning with Your Values

Living in alignment with your values is perhaps the most tranquil state one can achieve. It reduces internal conflicts and enhances decision-making clarity. Here, we'll discuss practical steps to ensure that your daily actions reflect your core values, leading to a more authentic and fulfilling life.

Small acts of self-care are potent tools that recalibrate our ability to cope with stress and enhance our capacity to enjoy life. They remind us that we have control over our day-to-day well-being and teach us that self-respect often starts with self-recognition—recognizing the need for rest, reflection, or even resistance against the grind culture.

The integration of these bite-sized practices serves as a foundation for a healthier mental state and a more balanced lifestyle. By starting small, these practices become sustainable rather than overwhelming additions to an already full schedule.

This chapter aims not just to educate, but also to inspire. It encourages you to step back, assess your needs honestly, and adopt small changes that honor those needs. Through this process, the overwhelming becomes manageable; fear transforms into courage—and ultimately leads you toward embracing a life you love filled with activities that enrich rather than drain you.

Discovering Your Strengths

Discovering your strengths is like unearthing hidden treasures within yourself. Each person harbors a unique set of skills, values, and passions, often buried under daily responsibilities and societal expectations. The first step in this exploration is to acknowledge that these treasures exist, waiting to be found.

To begin this journey, simple exercises such as listing achievements and moments of personal pride can be very enlightening. Reflecting on times when you felt most fulfilled or received commendation can provide clues to your inherent strengths. This factual approach offers a straightforward method to start recognizing what you naturally excel at.

Imagine yourself as a gardener, where your skills are like seeds. Some of these seeds sprout quickly, showing their potential early on, while others might need more care and time to reveal their true strength. The process of nurturing and understanding these skills requires patience and a gentle, yet consistent hand.

Another practical exercise involves seeking feedback from friends, family, or colleagues. Often, people around us can see strengths that we overlook in ourselves. This could be your ability to resolve conflicts, your creativity in problem-solving, or your knack for inspiring others. Gathering this external perspective can be incredibly insightful.

By engaging in these exercises, you begin to paint a clearer picture of your personal landscape of abilities. It's not just about identifying what you are good at, but also understanding how these skills align with your deeper values and passions, which brings a richer sense of fulfillment to your life.

Identifying your unique strengths is the first step towards personal growth and fulfillment.

Defining Personal Success

Success is a concept often shaped more by societal standards than by personal satisfaction. Many measure success by external achievements, such as career advancement, wealth, or social status. However, true success is deeply personal and can vary greatly from one person to another.

It's crucial to redefine success on your terms. Start by asking yourself what makes you genuinely happy and fulfilled. Is it the freedom to create, the time spent with loved ones, or the pursuit of knowledge and skills? This introspection shifts the focus from external accolades to internal satisfaction.

Consider success as a custom-made garment, tailored specifically for you. It should fit your personal aspirations perfectly, without being constrained by the one-size-fits-all approach often promoted by society. This analogy helps visualize the importance of a personalized definition of success.

Engage in self-reflection to determine what success means to you. Write down your vision of a successful life, considering all aspects—professional, personal, and spiritual. This exercise not only clarifies your goals but also motivates you to achieve them, aligned with your true desires.

Redefining success involves embracing failures as stepping stones. Each setback teaches valuable lessons that pave the way to future successes, tailored to your personal journey. This perspective encourages resilience and a positive attitude towards challenges.

The freedom to define your own success leads to a more authentic, satisfying life. It allows you to pursue goals that resonate with your values and aspirations, rather than chasing externally imposed benchmarks.

What does success truly mean to you, and how might redefining it lead to greater personal fulfillment?

The Self-Awareness Matrix

The Self-Awareness Matrix is a practical tool designed to enhance understanding and alignment of your strengths, values, and passions. It consists of four interconnected quadrants: Skills Identification, Values Assessment, Passion Exploration, and Vision Alignment. Each quadrant plays a crucial role in the journey towards self-awareness and personal success.

Skills Identification

In the Skills Identification quadrant, you are encouraged to list your unique abilities and reflect on past experiences where these skills were effectively utilized. This quadrant acts as the foundation of the matrix, supporting the other sections with a clear understanding of your competencies.

Values Assessment

Moving to the Values Assessment quadrant, this section helps clarify what truly matters to you. It includes a checklist of common values such as integrity, compassion, and innovation. Prioritizing these values allows you to see how they influence your daily decisions and long-term goals, providing a moral compass for your actions.

Passion Exploration

The Passion Exploration quadrant invites you to brainstorm activities that ignite your enthusiasm and make you lose track of time. This quadrant is vital for uncovering what truly drives and motivates you, which is essential for sustained engagement and satisfaction in your endeavors.

Vision Alignment

Finally, the Vision Alignment quadrant challenges you to define your ideal life vision. Here, you align your skills, values, and passions to create actionable steps toward achieving this vision. This comprehensive approach ensures that all aspects of your self-awareness contribute to a cohesive and fulfilling life strategy.

The dynamics of the Self-Awareness Matrix involve constant interaction between its components. For instance, a strength identified might lead to recognizing a related passion, or a deeply-held value might inspire a new vision for personal success. Over time, as you grow and evolve, the matrix adapts, offering new insights and directions.

In practical terms, this matrix serves as a roadmap, guiding you through the complexities of personal development and helping you navigate towards a life aligned with your true Self. It encourages continuous reflection and adjustment, ensuring that your path remains responsive to your evolving needs and aspirations.

The Self-Awareness Matrix not only aids in discovering and aligning your strengths, values, and

passions, but also fosters a deeper connection with yourself, leading to a more authentic and satisfying life.

As we wrap up this chapter, it's clear that recognizing your inherent strengths, defining personal success on your own terms, and aligning your daily life with your deepest values are crucial steps toward a more satisfying and authentic existence. Each of these areas not only contributes to a stronger sense of self-awareness, but also equips you with the tools to manage the pressures of everyday life more effectively.

Small acts of self-care are essential, particularly for those who feel overwhelmed by daily responsibilities. By incorporating manageable self-care practices such as brief meditations or short walks into your routine, you start to create a buffer against stress. These activities might seem small, but their effects are cumulative and significantly beneficial for mental health.

The process of identifying your strengths allows you to harness your capabilities in ways that are often overlooked when conforming to conventional markers of achievement. *When you define success on your own terms,* you prioritize goals that resonate with your personal aspirations and values, rather than those imposed by societal norms. This redefinition is liberating and aligns your efforts with what truly fulfills you.

Living in alignment with your values might sound straightforward, but it requires consistent reflection and adaptation. It's about making choices that resonate with your core beliefs and stepping back from those that don't. This alignment not only enhances your sense of authenticity, but also significantly improves your overall well-being.

Remember, the path to self-awareness is ongoing. Each step you take to understand and nurture your true Self adds a layer of confidence and clarity to your life. Start small, stay consistent, and watch as these efforts ripple out to affect all areas of your life positively.

By now, you should feel equipped to tackle the challenges that come with a busy life, using your newfound self-awareness as both shield and guide. Keep these strategies in mind as you continue through this book and beyond, and remember that every step forward is a step toward a more authentic, fulfilled Self.

Chapter Five

Your Voice Matters

Can Self-Care Truly Silence Guilt?

Margaret stood by the kitchen window, her hands cradled around a steaming mug of tea. The rain tapped a steady rhythm against the glass, echoing the cadence of her thoughts. She had always placed others before herself, a habit rooted deep in her upbringing. As she watched the droplets race each other down the window pane, she considered the advice from a book she had started reading—a book that proposed self-care as not just necessary but vital for her ability to care for others.

Her son's laughter floated from the living room, pulling her from her reverie. James was building a fort out of cushions and blankets, his imagination turning ordinary furniture into castles. Margaret smiled but felt the familiar pang of guilt at the thought of taking time for herself later that day—a planned walk alone in the park.

She remembered her mother's tireless hands, always occupied, always serving. Margaret had inherited that mantle of constant caregiving with pride, yet now it weighed on her like a heavy shawl. The book suggested re-framing self-care as an act not of selfishness but of recharging oneself to better serve loved ones. Could she adopt this new mindset?

As she sipped her tea, its warmth spreading through her, Margaret's mind wandered to last week's PTA meeting where she volunteered yet again for activities she had no bandwidth for. Her friend Lisa had whispered then, *"You need to take some time for yourself, too."* The words stung because they rang true.

The clock chimed, snapping Margaret back to reality. It was nearly time for James's lunch and then his piano lesson—another commitment made in hope it would forge his future. As she prepared sandwiches, slicing them precisely as he liked, she pondered how taking care of herself might actually make these moments—these slices of everyday life—more sustainable and perhaps even more joyful.

Could seeing self-care as essential help Margaret feel less guilty? Or is guilt an inevitable shadow cast by motherhood?

Silence Isn't Always Golden

In a world that often values self-sacrifice as a virtue, especially for women, the act of prioritizing one's own needs can feel uncomfortable, and even selfish. This chapter confronts the pervasive guilt associated with self-care head-on, advocating for a significant shift in perspective. It's about understanding that caring for oneself is not just beneficial, but crucial for sustaining our ability to care for others effectively.

Redefining Self-Care

The traditional concept of self-care often conjures images of temporary escapes from reality—think spa days or shopping sprees. However, genuine badass self-care is about more than just indulgence; it's about constructing a life where you don't frequently feel the need to escape from. This means setting boundaries, speaking up, and maintaining connections that reinforce rather than deplete your energy. By redefining self-care, we can dismiss the undue guilt often linked with putting ourselves first and recognize this practice as an essential part of our overall well-being, and reclaiming your own heart,s Badassery.

Overcoming the Guilt Barrier

For many, the idea of placing their needs on par with or even before those of others feels unnatural. This discomfort is often rooted in deep-seated beliefs about what it means to be a good mother, partner, friend, or employee—roles that traditionally come with expectations of constant availability and selflessness. Here, we explore why these beliefs take hold and how they can be reshaped to support a healthier, more balanced approach to personal well-being.

Tools for Assertive Expression

Silence can be golden, but not when it comes at the expense of your voice and needs. Learning to express oneself clearly and assertively is a key aspect of self-care. This section will introduce practical tools that help articulate needs without apology or excessive justification. Through simple yet effective communication techniques, readers will learn how to dismantle the fears associated with speaking up.

Cultivating Authentic Connections

Building relationships that truly support and enrich your life is another facet of badass self-care. We will look into how engaging authentically with others helps form a network of support that encourages mutual care. These connections are vital—they not only offer emotional support but also empower you to maintain your self-care practices without feeling isolated or selfish.

Practical Steps Forward

By integrating these insights into daily life, readers can start transforming their approach to personal care from one of guilt to one of empowerment. Each page aims to equip you with knowledge and strategies that foster an enduring change in how you view and practice self-care—a shift from viewing it as a luxury to understanding it as a necessity.

Through this exploration, The Courage To Be You" doesn't just propose a theory; it offers a path forward—a way to practically implement life-enhancing changes through self-awareness and assertive action. It's time to break free from the chains of guilt and embrace a life where you can thrive authentically, ensuring you're at your best not only for yourself but also for those around you.

Overcoming Silence

Have you ever found yourself in a conversation or meeting, bursting with thoughts or opinions, yet you choose silence? This common scenario reflects a larger issue where individuals, particularly women, hold back their voices due to various fears and societal expectations. Recognizing these moments is the first step toward change.

Imagine your thoughts as seeds in a garden. If never planted, they can't grow or bloom. Speaking up can be likened to planting these seeds where they can develop and enrich the environment. This analogy helps us see the potential lost when we keep our ideas to ourselves.

Statistics reveal that a significant number of women feel reluctant to speak in professional settings, fearing overstepping or being judged. This silence can stall career progression and personal growth. By identifying the roots of this hesitation, we can begin to address and nurture our confidence in our ideas and rights to share them.

The act of breaking free from the habit of silence involves both self-reflection and practical steps. Start by acknowledging the value of your opinions and the importance of contributing to discussions. This self-validation is crucial for building the courage to speak up.

Embrace the significance of your voice. Your ideas deserve a platform.

Speaking Up with Confidence

Speaking up confidently is not just about being loud; it's about clarity, assertiveness, and the ability to convey your thoughts effectively. To cultivate this skill, start by organizing your thoughts clearly before you speak. This preparation boosts confidence and ensures your message is understood.

Consider the power of a well-constructed building. Just as strong scaffolding supports a structure, a clear outline supports your words. This structure not only helps in delivering your message effectively but also fortifies your confidence as you speak.

Practical tools, such as the "assertive statement technique" help in this endeavor. Begin by stating your understanding of the situation, express your feelings about it, and conclude with your needs or desires. This method ensures that your communication is balanced and assertive.

Engaging in regular practice is key. Try starting with low-risk environments, like conversations with friends or family, and gradually progress to more challenging platforms such as meetings or public speaking.

Rhetorical questions can be powerful. For instance, have you ever considered the impact of your voice not just on others but on your own self-esteem? Speaking up can reinforce your self-worth and assert your place in any discourse.

How might your personal and professional life improve if you started expressing your thoughts more freely?

Building Supportive Connections

Creating meaningful relationships is essential for personal and professional growth. These connections are not just built on common interests, but on mutual respect and authentic interactions. When we engage genuinely with others, we lay a foundation for strong, supportive relationships.

Think of each relationship as a bridge. Just as a bridge connects two separate lands, relationships connect individuals, allowing for an exchange of ideas, support, and inspiration. The strength of these connections depends on the authenticity and effort invested by all parties involved.

It's important to be selective about whom you invest your time and energy in. Seek out people who not only inspire and motivate you but also provide constructive feedback and genuine support. These relationships should be empowering and reciprocal.

One practical step is to actively listen when engaging with others. This not only shows respect but also enhances your understanding of their perspectives, facilitating deeper connections.

Integrating the courage to speak up, the practice of self-care, and the cultivation of supportive relationships can radically transform your life. These steps foster a resilient, authentic Self, capable of thriving in any environment.

Through the insights shared in this chapter, we've explored the profound impact of giving voice to your thoughts and feelings. Recognizing and breaking free from moments of silence, confidently expressing yourself, and fostering supportive relationships are not merely acts of self-expression but foundational steps towards living authentically and fully.

Step-by-Step Process: Vocalize Your Value

Goal: To systematically increase your confidence in expressing your thoughts and building meaningful connections, thereby making your voice heard in all spheres of life.

1. Self-Reflection:

- **Timeframe:** 1 week
- Begin by documenting instances where you felt unable to speak your mind. Write down the

scenario, how you felt, and why you might have hesitated. This process will help you identify and understand patterns that have silenced you.

2. Practice in Safe Spaces:

- **Timeframe:** 2 weeks
- Start small by sharing your opinions during casual conversations with friends or family. Choose topics you're passionate about to make this exercise easier and more engaging.

3. Gradual Exposure:

- **Timeframe:** 1 month
- Increase the stakes gradually by expressing your views in more formal settings like workplace meetings or community gatherings. Aim to speak up at least once in each discussion.

4. Seek Feedback:

- **Timeframe:** Ongoing
- After each interaction, seek constructive feedback from trusted peers or mentors. This will help you refine your communication style and approach.

1. **Build and Engage with Your Community:**

- **Timeframe:** Ongoing
- Actively seek out and participate in groups that share your interests or support personal growth, such as workshops or local clubs. These connections can provide encouragement and further opportunities for practice.

5. Reflect and Celebrate:

- **Timeframe:** Ongoing
- Regularly review your progress and take note of any positive outcomes or shifts in your confidence. Celebrating these victories, big or small, reinforces your capability and encourages continual growth.

6. Challenge Yourself:

- **Timeframe:** Ongoing
- As your confidence builds, challenge yourself to tackle more significant issues or public speaking opportunities. Each challenge is a step forward in using your voice effectively.

This process is designed to be flexible, allowing adjustments based on personal growth and comfort. It's structured to provide a clear path toward not just speaking up but being heard and valued in every conversation.

By integrating these practices into your daily life, you will find that prioritizing self-expression becomes less about overcoming guilt and more about recognizing its necessity for personal and communal well-being. Your voice is not just a personal power—it is an essential tool for creating change in your life and the lives of those around you. As you continue to make your voice matter, remember that each step forward enhances not only your own life, but also empowers those around you to find their voices too.

Chapter Six

Silencing the Inner Critic

Can a Circle of Friends Shield You from the World's Sharp Corners?

Amelia stood at the edge of the park, watching children scatter like autumn leaves under a brisk wind. The sun dipped low, brushing the horizon with strokes of orange and pink, and she felt that familiar tightening in her chest—the weight of eyes, real or imagined, scrutinizing her every choice.

She had moved to this small town just a few months ago, fleeing from a city that had grown too cold and indifferent for her tender heart. Here, in this close-knit community where everyone knew each other's grandparents and first pets, she had hoped to find shelter from the harsh judgments that had shadowed her elsewhere.

As she walked along the gravel path, her thoughts drifted to last week's town meeting. She recalled standing up to speak about the new community garden project, her voice trembling slightly as she explained its benefits. Afterwards, Mrs. Harmon from across the street had squeezed her arm and whispered, *"Don't mind old Jerry; he criticizes everything not born from his own thoughts."* That small gesture felt like a warm blanket on a chilly evening.

The crisp sound of leaves crushing underfoot pulled Amelia back from her reverie. She watched an elderly couple pass by; their hands intertwined, seemingly unbothered by the world around them. How did they do it? How did they find such ease in this maze of human expectations?

Her phone buzzed—a message from Laura, inviting her to join a few neighbors for dinner. Amelia hesitated; gatherings were still battlefields in some way, places where one wrong word could turn into whispers behind closed doors. Yet there was also laughter there, shared stories spilling over plates of homemade food.

She made up her mind as another message popped up: *"We'd love to have you! Don't worry about bringing anything but your smile."*

Maybe this was it—her buffer against those invisible arrows shot from unseen bows. Perhaps community wasn't just about living side by side but standing shoulder to shoulder too.

As she turned towards home to change before dinner, Amelia wondered if every step taken in trust was another brick laid in the fortress protecting one from judgment's reach.

Could acceptance within a few truly overshadow the scrutiny of many?

The Strength of Community: Your Shield Against the Inner Critic

In the pursuit of authentic self-expression, the loudest barrier is often the voice inside our own head. This internal dialogue can be harsh and unrelenting, rooted in fear and amplified by external judgment. In this chapter, we explore how building a supportive community not only challenges but also quiets this inner critic, offering a solid foundation from which personal growth can flourish. The support of compassionate peers acts as a buffer against the sharp edges of self-doubt and societal critique.

Identifying the Roots of Negative Self-Talk

Firstly, understanding where these critical voices come from is crucial. They are often a combination of past experiences, societal expectations, and even the media we consume. Recognizing that these voices are not inherently truths but rather echoes of external opinions can be liberating. It's important to discern which aspects of this negativity truly belong to us and which are imposed from outside sources.

Reframing Our Inner Narrative

The power to reframe our internal narrative lies in actively choosing which voices to amplify and which to challenge. By consciously replacing self-doubt with affirmative beliefs, we begin to reshape our self-perception. This doesn't mean ignoring all criticism, but rather learning to extract useful feedback while discarding destructive negativity.

The Role of Community in Fostering Belief

Here lies the strength of community. When surrounded by individuals who uplift rather than undermine, it becomes easier to believe in our own values. A supportive group provides not just affirmation but also perspective—helping us see ourselves through a lens unclouded by our harshest judgments.

Strategies for Building Self-Belief

Building on a foundation of understanding and reframing, we then turn to concrete strategies for enhancing self-belief. These include setting achievable goals, celebrating small victories, and actively seeking environments that reinforce positive self-regard. Through these actions, trust in one's own abilities grows, bolstered by communal support and individual resilience.

Practical Applications and Real-Life Successes

The chapter will not only discuss these concepts, but also provide practical applications through real-life examples. Stories of individuals who have successfully silenced their inner critics through community support will serve as both inspiration and blueprint for readers looking to do the same.

A Call to Action: Cultivating Your Community

Finally, cultivating such a community does not happen by chance; it requires intentionality. Engaging with groups that share similar values or aspirations can dramatically alter one's journey towards self-acceptance. Whether it's through local clubs, online forums, or professional networks—the goal is to connect with others who encourage personal authenticity over conformity.

Through understanding negative self-talk, reframing our personal narratives, and actively building communities that uplift, this chapter aims to guide readers toward a more confident and self-assured existence. Herein lies the potential for a life lived with courage—a life where the inner critic no longer holds sway over our choices or our dreams.

Understanding Negative Self-Talk

Negative self-talk often stems from the deep-seated belief systems we develop early in life. From a young age, many of us are inundated with messages about how we should behave, what we should achieve, and the ways we need to present ourselves to the world. These messages can originate from family, culture, media, and personal experiences. Over time, they form a persistent internal voice that critiques our every action.

Imagine your mind as a garden, where each thought is a seed. Negative self-talk is like weeds that can overrun this garden if left unchecked. They grow wildly, based on the seeds sown by doubt and criticism absorbed over the years. Just as weeds can choke the life out of flowers and vegetables, unchecked negative thoughts can stifle your growth and happiness.

It's crucial to recognize that this inner critic isn't an accurate reflection of reality or your potential. Often, it's a collection of external voices and past disappointments that have embedded themselves into your psyche. Identifying these sources of negative self-talk is the first step towards silencing them.

Understanding why this inner critic is so pervasive helps in managing it effectively. It's persistent because it's familiar, often echoing the tones of influential people from our past. However, just because a voice is loud doesn't mean it is right. By recognizing these patterns, we can begin to question and ultimately silence the critic.

The key is to recognize the origins of your inner critic to silence it effectively.

Reframing the Narrative

To reframe the narrative of your inner critic, start by challenging the accuracy of its statements. Often, this voice generalizes isolated setbacks as never-ending failures. For example, a single mistake at work becomes an eternal label of incompetence. This isn't just unhelpful; it's an unrealistic and harsh interpretation of events.

Reframing involves flipping the script. Instead of accepting the critic's harsh judgments, ask yourself: "Is this really true? Are there instances where I have succeeded in similar situations?" This type of questioning can reveal that the narrative you've been repeating to yourself isn't entirely accurate.

Consider your thoughts as different radio stations. Just as you would change the station from a channel that only plays songs you dislike to one that plays your favorites, you can switch your mental narrative from criticism to encouragement. This shift doesn't happen overnight, but with practice, tuning into a more supportive frequency becomes easier.

Incorporating positive affirmations is another powerful tool. Instead of saying *"I always mess up,"* try affirming *"I am capable of learning and growing from my mistakes."* These affirmations are not about convincing yourself of something untrue, but reinforcing the positive aspects of your reality.

Can you imagine how much more peaceful your mind would be if it were your ally rather than your critic?

Building Self-Belief

Building self-belief is similar to constructing a house. It requires a solid foundation, reliable tools, and regular maintenance. The foundation of self-belief is built on understanding and managing negative self-talk, as discussed earlier. The tools are the techniques we use, such as reframing negative thoughts and practicing positive affirmations.

A key strategy in fostering self-confidence is setting small, achievable goals. These act as stepping stones that gradually build your trust in your abilities. Each achievement, no matter how small, is a brick in the structure of your self-belief. Celebrating these victories can reinforce your confidence and motivate you to tackle larger challenges.

Another effective method is to keep a journal where you record successes and positive feedback. This can serve as a tangible reminder of your capabilities, especially when your inner critic tries to downplay your achievements. Over time, this record will provide undeniable evidence of your growth and resilience.

By understanding the nature of negative self-talk, learning to reframe the narrative, and actively building self-belief, you create a supportive inner environment that encourages personal growth and resilience.

In this chapter, we have explored the pervasive issue of negative self-talk, learning to recognize its origins and understanding its implications on our confidence and self-image. We've tackled strategies to reframe our internal narratives, shifting from self-doubt to more positive and supportive beliefs. Furthermore, we discussed building self-belief through practical, actionable strategies that foster trust in our abilities.

The process outlined in this chapter is crucial because it directly addresses the barriers that prevent us from embracing a life we love. It's not just about silencing that inner critic; it's about transforming the way we interact with ourselves on a daily basis. By actively engaging in reframing our thoughts and reinforcing our self-belief, we initiate a powerful change in our mindset.

Community support plays a critical role in this transformation. It acts as a buffer against the harsh judgments we often fear from the outside world. When we surround ourselves with people who uplift and support us, we are not only shielded, but are also empowered to act without fear of external criticism. This supportive network is vital as it provides not just reassurance, but also accountability as we strive to replace old habits of self-criticism with new patterns of self-support.

Practical examples from real-life scenarios show us that these strategies are not just theoretical but highly effective. Individuals who have embraced these methods report a significant boost in their confidence and a decrease in the impact of negative self-talk. These stories serve as proof that with the right tools and support, anyone can overcome the internal barriers that stand in the way of their potential.

By investing in our relationship with ourselves and nurturing connections with others who encourage and support our growth, we lay down the foundation for lasting personal development. It's essential to remember that this process is ongoing—a continual practice of affirming our worth and capabilities.

As you move forward, recall the strategies discussed here and actively apply them. Challenge the critical voices within, replace them with affirmations of your strength and value, and lean on your community when doubt creeps back in. With consistent practice, you'll find that what once seemed like insurmountable self-doubt becomes manageable and eventually, much quieter.

Embrace these changes not just as steps toward personal improvement, but as essential elements in leading a life filled with confidence, authenticity, and joy. Remember, the goal is to thrive authentically, equipped with tools that not only combat negative self-talk, but also build a resilient, confident self-image.

Chapter Seven

Prioritizing You Without Guilt

Can Rediscovered Passions Rekindle a Forgotten Self?

Ella stood at the kitchen window, her gaze drifting past the steam that curled up from the teapot, settling on the frosted garden beyond. The gray light of the early morning cast long shadows across the snow, painting a quiet picture that contrasted sharply with the turmoil inside her. Once vibrant and full of purpose, she now often felt like just a spectator in her own life, watching days blend into one another as she tended to everyone's needs but her own.

Her thoughts were interrupted by the shrill cries of her young twins demanding breakfast. As she turned towards them, a half-forgotten image flickered through her mind: herself, years ago, brush in hand, lost in the creation of a vast, colorful canvas. Art had been her sanctuary, a vivid expression of identity now buried under layers of motherly duties and office tasks. The memory was like a whisper from someone she used to know very well but hadn't seen in years.

Later that day, walking through the park wrapped in her thick scarf and coat against the biting wind, Ella watched other walkers; some solitary figures with dogs trotting beside them, others laughing groups sharing warmth and stories. She noticed how each person's breath came out in visible puffs against the cold air—each one living their moment, perhaps closer to their essence than she felt to hers.

At home again, surrounded by quiet as the children napped and her partner read in another room, Ella stood before an old easel found tucked away in the attic earlier that day. Touching its rough wood brought back more flashes—joyful hours mixing paints, framing emotions on canvas—and with them an ache for that lost part of herself. She wiped off dust from an old paintbox; its colors still bright but untouched for so long they seemed almost hesitant under her fingers.

As she tentatively began to stroke blue onto a blank canvas set before her—the first tentative step toward reclaiming herself through forgotten passion—a question lingered silently: Could these silent colors sing loud enough to bring back who she once was?

Rediscover Yourself: No Apologies Necessary

In a world where women often juggle multiple roles—caretaker, professional, partner, parent—their own identities can become overshadowed by the relentless demands of daily life. **"Prioritizing You Without Guilt"** is about reversing this trend, focusing on rekindling your personal passions as a pathway to rediscovering and strengthening your sense of Self. This shift is not just beneficial, but essential for your overall happiness and effectiveness in every role you play.

Often, prioritizing oneself is mistakenly viewed as selfish or indulgent, especially when others depend on you. However, this chapter will dismantle these misconceptions and illustrate how integrating self-care into your routine is crucial for sustaining both personal well-being and healthy relationships. By understanding **the value of self-care**, you'll see why putting yourself first at times is a necessity, not a luxury.

Creating a **custom self-care plan** may sound daunting, but it's about simple, achievable steps that fit seamlessly into your life. This isn't about overhauling your routine overnight, but identifying what replenishes your energy and makes you feel whole. Whether it's picking up an old hobby or discovering a new interest, these activities are the building blocks of a happier, more fulfilled you.

Consistency in self-care is where many stumble—initial enthusiasm wanes, or guilt creeps in. Here, we'll explore strategies to maintain consistency in your self-care practices without feeling selfish or neglectful. It's about setting realistic expectations and gently integrating these practices into your life, so they become as regular as any other essential activity.

The real-life examples sprinkled throughout this discussion are not just stories; they are proof that these strategies work. They offer both inspiration and a blueprint for what can be achieved when you dare to put yourself on your own to-do list.

As we unpack these concepts, remember: prioritizing yourself isn't just about finding time for a spa day—it's about cultivating a mindset where your needs matter and acting on this consistently. It's about making room for growth, joy, and peace in your life that radiates out to those around you.

By the end of this chapter, the hope is not only to have equipped you with practical tools but also to have shifted your perspective on self-care from optional to essential. Reclaiming parts of yourself that were lost in everyday demands allows you to live not just adequately but vibrantly—making the rest of life's challenges more manageable and enjoyable. So let's begin this critical conversation on how to care deeply for ourselves without an ounce of guilt and getting one-step closer to reclaiming your own badass Self.

The Value of Self-Care

Understanding the importance of self-care is crucial in a world where demands often drown out personal needs. Self-care is not merely a trend; it's an essential component of a healthy lifestyle. It involves any activity that we do deliberately to take care of our physical, mental, emotional, and spiritual health. Although it's a simple concept in theory, it's something we very often overlook.

Imagine your energy as a battery that needs recharging. Just like you wouldn't expect your phone to run indefinitely without plugging it in, you can't expect your body and mind to continue operating at their best without recharging through self-care. This analogy highlights the necessity of self-care as a fundamental part of maintaining our health and well-being.

Good self-care is key to improved mood and reduced anxiety. It's also key to a good relationship with oneself and others. By keeping your body and mind well, you're better equipped to live your life to the fullest. Neglecting self-care can lead to overwhelming stress, fatigue, body aches and a decrease in the ability to effectively take care of yourself and others.

Consider self-care as an investment in yourself. When you're well-cared for, the likelihood of feeling happy and healthy increases, and you're more capable of managing the stress that life throws your way. Furthermore, when you feel better, you make better choices around your needs and the needs of others.

Self-care is vital for building resilience towards those stressors in life that you can't eliminate.

Creating a Custom Self-Care Plan

Designing a badass self-care plan tailored to your individual needs can seem daunting, but it's a powerful step toward a happier, healthier you. A custom self-care plan helps you identify what you need to stay physically, mentally, emotionally, and spiritually balanced. It's about knowing what makes you thrive, not just what keeps you functioning.

A well-crafted self-care plan acts as a roadmap. Think of it as creating a garden; different plants need different amounts of sunlight, water, and nutrients. Similarly, each aspect of your well-being needs different kinds of care. Recognizing these needs allows you to nurture them effectively.

How do you currently care for yourself?

This question invites you to evaluate your current practices and adjust them to better serve your needs. It's not about overhauling your life but integrating practices that align with your personal well-being. It could be something as simple as scheduling time to read a book, taking a long walk, or prioritizing sleep.

The plan should be flexible—adaptable to your changing needs and circumstances. Life is unpredictable, and your self-care needs to bend rather than break under pressure. Consistency is key, but so is adaptability, allowing your plan to evolve as you do.

By regularly engaging in self-care practices that you've chosen for yourself, you reinforce a positive relationship with yourself. Each act of self-care is a reaffirmation of your worth and a step towards a more balanced life.

Could crafting your badass self-care plan be the key to a rejuvenated sense of self?

Embracing Consistency

The challenge with self-care is not just in starting, but in maintaining consistency. Regular self-care is not about indulgence but about making a commitment to stay healthy and balanced. It's about making small, consistent choices that boost your well-being every day.

The Guilt-Alleviation Self-Care Ladder

Rung #1: Basic Self-Care

The first level involves simple acts like staying hydrated and ensuring you get enough sleep. These foundational practices are often overlooked, but are crucial for maintaining basic health.

Rung #2: Intentional Self-Care

Here, you introduce activities like mindful breathing or scheduled breaks during your day. This rung encourages you to be more deliberate with your self-care, setting aside specific times for it.

Rung #3: Relational Self-Care

Expanding your self-care to include social interactions, this rung encourages reaching out to friends or participating in community activities. It highlights the importance of support networks in personal well-being.

Rung #4: Structured Self-Care

This involves setting up routines that support your self-care goals, such as weekly classes or dedicated *"me time."* This structure helps to ensure that self-care is a regular part of your schedule.

Rung #5: Holistic Self-Care

The final rung integrates mental, physical, emotional, and spiritual wellness strategies. This comprehensive approach might include therapy, fitness regimes, or creative pursuits, fostering an overall balance.

Each rung of the ladder not only supports the next but also builds on the previous, creating a holistic and sustainable model of self-care. This progression ensures that self-care becomes a natural and guilt-free element of your daily life.

By integrating these practices into your life, you create a self-sustaining cycle of badass self-care that enhances every aspect of your being.

As we wrap up this chapter, it's essential to recognize that prioritizing yourself is not just beneficial—it's necessary. Through understanding the value of self-care, developing a custom plan, and embracing consistency, you lay the groundwork for a more fulfilled and authentic life.

Self-care is fundamental to your well-being and the quality of your relationships. It's not about indulgence; it's about making sure you're physically, mentally, emotionally and spiritually equipped to handle life's challenges. When you take care of yourself, you're in a better position to care for others and engage with the world around you.

Creating a personalized self-care plan allows you to integrate activities that resonate with your personal passions into your daily routine. This is not about following a generic template, but about crafting a plan that aligns with your unique life circumstances and goals. Whether it's taking up an old hobby, dedicating time to read, or simply taking a walk, these activities are vital for reconnecting with yourself.

Consistency in self-care practices ensures that these efforts are effective and lasting. It's one thing to recognize the importance of self-care; it's another to live it out daily. Regularly engaging in your self-care routine solidifies it as a natural part of your life, not just a sporadic luxury.

By reintegrating passion-led activities into your life, you do more than just fill your time with enjoyable tasks—you *reignite your sense of identity*. This revitalization of self can boost your confidence significantly, providing you with the clarity to see your own worth and the courage to express it.

Remember, making yourself a priority is a practical approach to a healthier and more vibrant life. As you move forward, carry with you the strategies from this chapter, knowing that they are designed to support your personal growth and help you thrive authentically. Each step you take in this direction not only enhances your own life but also sets a powerful example for those around you. Keep pushing the boundaries of what you believe is possible for yourself. Your commitment to this process is not just rewarding; it's transformative.

Chapter Eight

Setting Boundaries That Stick

Can One Truly Find Peace in Saying No?

Clara stood at her kitchen window, watching the early morning light bathe her small garden in a soft, golden glow. It was a Saturday, yet her mind raced through the list of obligations she had said yes to: a brunch with colleagues, a midday meeting for the local book club she had never really wanted to join, and an evening helping her sister organize a family gathering. Each commitment nibbled at her peace.

As she turned from the window to start her day, the phone rang. It was Rachel, her old friend from college, asking if Clara could assist with a community project next weekend. Clara paused, spoon in hand, stirring her tea absentmindedly as she listened. Her heart sank; another slice of her time was being requested, yet something inside her stirred today.

The kitchen filled with the rich aroma of tea as Clara's mind wandered to last Wednesday's therapy session where they discussed boundary setting. *"It's about preserving your own energy,"* her therapist had reminded gently. The words echoed in Clara's thoughts now as she gazed at the steam rising from her cup like tiny spirits breaking free.

Outside, a gentle breeze played with the leaves of the oak tree that stood watch over her home. It seemed to sway in rhythm with Clara's deepening breaths as she prepared to respond to Rachel. The leaves rustled their encouragement.

"I'm sorry, Rachel," Clara finally spoke into the phone with a surprising calmness and clarity that startled even herself. *"I can't commit to that right now."*

Silence followed—not awkward but open and expansive like the sky after a storm clears.

Rachel responded kindly, and they concluded their conversation with promises to catch up more personally soon—a chat without requests or expectations hanging over them like heavy clouds.

The rest of Clara's morning passed quietly, with each task feeling lighter than before. As noon approached and sunlight spilled over into every corner of rooms usually dimmed by curtains drawn tight against intrusions—both sunlight and obligations—Clara felt an unfamiliar ease.

She sat down on the couch now flooded with warmth from outside, and let out a sigh that seemed held for years—a prisoner of politeness now set free by boundaries newly drawn.

As birds sang their midday songs outside, unfettered by any duty other than their own survival and joyous expression, one wonders: can setting boundaries not only preserve energy but also reclaim it? How much life awaits in those moments reclaimed from unyielding obligation?

Are You In Charge of Your Own Life?

In a world where saying 'yes' is often automated, learning the art of saying 'no' can be revolutionary. This chapter explores the critical skill of setting boundaries—a fundamental step towards mental health and badass self-care. For many women, the challenge isn't just about managing time; it's about reclaiming it. By setting firm boundaries, you not only protect your energy, but also open doors to personal growth and fulfillment.

Recognizing when and where your limits are being tested is the first step toward taking control. It's common to feel a sense of obligation towards our loved ones or a need to meet workplace demands at the cost of our well-being. This chapter will help you identify these moments before they lead to burnout.

The Art of Clear Communication

Setting boundaries is one thing; communicating them effectively is another. It’s not just about what you say but how you say it. This section will provide clear strategies for expressing your needs assertively and respectfully, ensuring that your voice is heard without guilt or apology. The goal is to make your interactions as straightforward as possible, reducing the stress that often comes with confrontation.

Sustaining boundaries can be even more challenging than setting them, especially in the face of resistance or guilt. Here, we will discuss how to maintain your stance over time and handle boundary breaches with confidence. We'll explore practical ways to reinforce your boundaries without constant conflict, allowing for healthier relationships both personally and professionally.

Each section includes real-life scenarios that illustrate common boundary challenges and effective solutions. These stories not only demonstrate the struggles many women face, but also celebrate their successes in overcoming them.

Remember, setting boundaries isn't a one-time task—it's a continuous process that requires persistence and commitment. But with the right tools and mindset, it's entirely achievable.

This chapter doesn't just advise—it equips you with the necessary tools to act. By embracing these principles, you're not just setting limits; you're paving the way for a more balanced, energized life where *your needs* come first.

So take charge today; define what matters most to you and build your life around it. Your mental health, time, and energy are precious—treat them that way!

Recognizing Boundary Issues

Many of us struggle with setting boundaries because the concept itself can feel unnatural or rigid. We might worry about hurting others' feelings or fear rejection. However, recognizing where we have boundary issues is the first critical step in reclaiming control of our lives. By identifying these areas, we can start to understand how they impact our mental health and personal growth.

Think of boundaries like the walls of a house. They keep the good in and the bad out. When the walls are weak or non-existent, anything and everything can enter, leaving us feeling overwhelmed and unprotected. This lack of boundaries can lead to stress, anxiety, and a sense of loss of control. It's important to understand that having strong, clear boundaries is the same as having a well-secured home.

Often, we inherit our boundary-setting abilities from our upbringing. If you grew up in an environment where boundaries were either too strict or too loose, you might find yourself replicating similar patterns in adulthood. This realization is crucial because it offers a starting point for change. Knowing the root of our boundary issues can lead us to a better understanding of our current relationships and work dynamics.

Setting boundaries is not about being selfish; it's about self-respect. It involves understanding what you need to thrive and communicating these needs to those around you. When we fail to set boundaries, we allow others to dictate our actions, choices, and emotions. Recognizing this can be a powerful motivator for change, as it highlights the direct link between personal boundaries and personal freedom.

Recognizing where you struggle with boundary setting is crucial for personal development and mental well-being.

Communicating Boundaries Effectively

Communicating boundaries effectively is more than just stating what you are uncomfortable with; it's about being clear, assertive, and respectful. It requires confidence and the belief that your needs are important. The way we communicate our boundaries directly affects how well they are respected and upheld.

One effective strategy is the use of *"I"* statements. Instead of saying *"You make me feel overwhelmed,"* rephrase it to *"I feel overwhelmed when too many demands are placed on me at once."* This method of communication reduces defensiveness and keeps the focus on your feelings and needs.

Imagine a scenario where your friend asks you to help organize a community event. You already feel stretched thin. Here, an effective boundary might be, *"I appreciate your thinking of me, but I need to focus on my current commitments."* This response is clear and respectful, asserting your limits without guilt.

Moreover, timing and tone play crucial roles in how your boundaries are received. Delivering your message in a calm and positive tone when both parties are relaxed can lead to better understanding and respect for your boundaries.

Consider the effectiveness of rehearsing your boundary statements before delivering them. Just as actors rehearse their lines to ensure a natural flow during the performance, practicing your boundaries can make the actual conversation feel more comfortable and confident.

How might changing your approach to communicating boundaries alter your relationships and self-perception?

Sustaining Your Boundaries

Maintaining boundaries is an ongoing process that often requires us to reinforce them repeatedly. It's not enough to set them once and expect them to hold permanently, especially in long-standing relationships where old habits die hard.

A practical step in sustaining your boundaries is to regularly assess and adjust them as needed. Life changes, and so do our needs and relationships. An annual review of your boundaries, much like a performance review at work, can help keep them relevant and effective.

Another key strategy is to cultivate a support system that respects and upholds your boundaries. Surround yourself with people who understand the importance of boundaries and encourage you to maintain yours. This support can be crucial in moments of doubt or when you face pushback.

Remember, it's normal for boundaries to be tested. Each time they are challenged is an opportunity to strengthen them. Respond consistently and calmly reaffirm your boundaries each time they are pushed. This consistency sends a clear message that you are serious about your limits.

Setting boundaries is a vital skill for mental health and self-care. Recognizing boundary issues, communicating them effectively, and sustaining them are all critical steps in ensuring they serve their purpose.

As we wrap up this chapter, it's clear that the ability to set and sustain boundaries is not just a skill—it's a necessity for mental health and personal growth. Recognizing where boundary issues lie, articulating your limits clearly, and maintaining those boundaries consistently are critical steps in managing life's demands without sacrificing your well-being.

Recognizing boundary issues is the first step towards change. When you understand where you've struggled with setting limits, you can begin to address these challenges directly. This awareness is crucial, as it sets the foundation for developing stronger interpersonal skills and self-respect.

Communicating boundaries effectively involves more than just saying 'no'—it's about expressing your needs clearly and respectfully. This ensures that your relationships are built on mutual respect and understanding. Practical examples, like using *"I"* statements and being specific about what is acceptable, can transform difficult conversations into opportunities for growth.

Sustaining your boundaries is perhaps the most challenging part. It requires consistency, courage, and the willingness to revisit and adjust boundaries as circumstances change. Strategies such as regular self-reflection and seeking support when needed are vital in making sure your boundaries are not just set but also respected long-term.

By integrating these practices into your daily life, you create space for personal development and healthier relationships. Remember, setting boundaries is a form of self-care that allows you to honor your needs and feelings as valid and important. It's not about building walls, but about nurturing the courage to respect yourself and demand that same respect from others.

As you move forward, keep in mind that boundary setting is a dynamic process that benefits greatly from continuous learning and adaptation. Each conversation and decision is a step towards a more balanced and fulfilling life. So, stay committed to practicing these skills, and watch as your life transforms into one where you can truly thrive authentically.

Chapter Nine

Taking Inspired Action

Can Mindfulness Reveal the Path to One's True Desires?

Amelia sat by the window, her gaze drifting over the bustling street below, filled with the early stirrings of city life. The sun peeked through a blanket of clouds, casting a warm glow that danced on her skin. She held a journal, its pages worn from frequent use, each line a testament to her search for clarity. Today, she wrote about last night's meditation, which had been particularly revealing.

As she penned down her thoughts, Amelia recalled the tightness in her chest during the session. It was a physical manifestation of her current predicament—stuck in a job that paid well but starved her soul. The more she meditated, the more she realized this discomfort wasn't just fatigue; it was dissatisfaction whispering through her bones.

Her phone buzzed beside her—a reminder of an upcoming meeting. She sighed and closed her journal with gentle finality. Standing up, she felt the weight of decision pressing down on her shoulders as she prepared for another day at work.

At the office, Amelia's fingers danced across the keyboard with mechanical precision while her mind wandered back to this morning's journal entry. Her boss noticed her distant look and asked if everything was alright. She smiled and nodded, not wanting to reveal the turmoil inside.

Lunchtime brought reprieve as Amelia escaped to the park across from their building. She sat under an old oak tree whose leaves whispered secrets only they knew. Here in this quiet place, surrounded by nature's simple beauty, thoughts flowed freely.

She wondered about what truly made her happy—writing poetry and helping others discover their own creative voices. Could she turn this passion into a sustainable career? Was it foolish to even consider such a change at this stage in her life?

The cool breeze brushed against Amelia's face as if urging her to listen closer to what lay within her heart rather than what echoed around from society's expectations.

What might happen if Amelia trusted these insights revealed through mindfulness? Could they indeed guide her toward a life more aligned with who she really is?

When Intention Meets Action: The Gateway to Authentic Living

In a world that often praises the hustle, it's easy to overlook the profound power of thoughtful reflection and deliberate action. Yet, as we explore in this section, mindfulness is not just about being present—it's a strategic tool for unraveling the complexities of your aspirations and transforming them into tangible outcomes.

Mindfulness serves as a foundation for deepening self-awareness, which is critical in understanding one's true desires and needs. By engaging in regular practices such as meditation and journaling, you are not simply participating in a trendy wellness activity; you are setting the stage for a transformative process that aligns your daily actions with your deepest values.

Breaking Down Your Goals

Imagine facing a towering mountain—intimidating and seemingly insurmountable. Now picture yourself mapping out a path, marking small achievable milestones along the way. This visualization process mirrors how breaking down overwhelming goals into manageable steps can significantly ease the journey towards achieving them. It's not just about making progress, but making progress in a way that is sustainable and aligned with who you truly are.

Breaking Down Your Goals

When faced with a hefty goal, the process can often feel as daunting as standing at the foot of a mountain. It's easy to get overwhelmed by the sheer scale of the aspirations we set for ourselves. However, the key to managing this is to break down your goals into smaller, more manageable steps. This approach transforms what seems like an insurmountable task into a series of achievable actions.

Imagine each goal as a puzzle. Initially, it's a whole image that might seem complex and difficult to solve. But once you start separating out the pieces and finding where each one fits, the picture becomes clearer and easier to complete. This is exactly how we should handle our goals. By deconstructing them into smaller, specific tasks, we make the goal less intimidating and more attainable.

Setting these smaller objectives also allows for regular assessment and adjustment. It's crucial to track progress and make tweaks to your plans as necessary. This keeps you flexible and responsive to any changes in your circumstances or insights you might gain along the way.

Another vital element is to set deadlines for these smaller tasks. This creates urgency and a sense of purpose, driving you forward. Deadlines help you avoid the pitfall of procrastination and maintain your focus on the goal ahead.

By breaking down your goals into manageable steps, you make the path to success clearer and less daunting.

Building Momentum

Consistency is key in any endeavor, but maintaining it requires more than just willpower; it demands motivation. Strategies to build and sustain momentum are crucial because they transform the daunting into the doable. By nurturing your motivation through celebrating small victories and maintaining a supportive environment, you create a self-reinforcing cycle of actions that propel you forward.

Maintaining momentum is critical once you've started on your goal-achieving path. It's like keeping the wheels turning on a bicycle; the moment you stop pedaling, you start to slow down and eventually come to a halt. To keep moving, you need consistent effort and strategies to stay motivated.

One effective strategy is to celebrate small victories. Each small task completed on the way to your larger goal deserves recognition. These celebrations reinforce positive behavior and keep you motivated. They remind you that progress, no matter how minor, is still progress.

Do you remember the last time you felt a rush of excitement after accomplishing a task? That feeling is a powerful motivator, and by recognizing and celebrating these moments, you fuel your journey forward. It's about finding joy in the journey itself, not just the destination.

Visual reminders can also serve as significant motivators. Whether it's a progress chart on your wall or a series of notes in your planner, having tangible signs of your progress can boost your motivation. They serve as constant reminders of what you've achieved and what's still ahead.

Consistency is another cornerstone of building momentum. It's not just about working hard; it's about working smart and regularly. This means setting aside time each day or each week to focus on your goals, creating a routine that supports your aspirations.

What could happen if you took a moment right now to celebrate your most recent achievement and allowed that success to propel you forward?

Overcoming Obstacles

In the pursuit of any goal, obstacles are inevitable. They can either stall our progress or serve as stepping stones, depending on how we handle them. The ability to navigate these challenges is crucial in keeping the momentum towards achieving your goals.

Consider obstacles as detours, not roadblocks. A detour might slow you down, but it doesn't mean you won't reach your destination. It's an opportunity to explore different routes, perhaps even discovering a more scenic or quicker path than the one you originally planned.

Adapting to setbacks involves a flexible mindset. Instead of getting frustrated or giving up when faced with a challenge, ask yourself what can be learned or gained from this situation. Each obstacle is a chance to grow stronger and become more adept at dealing with future challenges.

It's also beneficial to seek support when faced with difficult situations. This could be from friends, family, or even professional advisors. Sharing your struggles can lighten your emotional load and provide new perspectives on tackling the issue.

By breaking down your goals, staying motivated, and overcoming obstacles, you create a solid foundation for personal and professional growth.

These strategies not only facilitate reaching your aspirations, but also promote a deeper understanding of your capabilities and potential. Each step forward, no matter how small, is a crucial part of the larger picture of your personal development.

As I stated earlier, setbacks are an inevitable part of any process. However, the ability to navigate these challenges effectively can be learned and refined over time. Tools and strategies discussed here are designed to help you turn obstacles into opportunities, ensuring that each step back is followed by two steps forward.

In synthesizing mindfulness with action, this chapter aims to guide you through structuring your aspirations into achievable objectives, fostering persistent motivation, and developing resilience against inevitable setbacks. The focus is on practicality—implementing mindful techniques to cultivate an environment where inspired action thrives.

By integrating these practices into your life, you not only enhance your capacity for self-awareness, but also equip yourself with the tools necessary to act on this heightened understanding. It's about creating a feedback loop where mindfulness informs action and action, in turn, deepens mindfulness.

Your path to personal fulfillment involves recognizing that each mindful step is both a destination and part of a greater process. It's here that you find the clarity to see beyond fear and the courage to embrace life passionately and authentically.

This approach does not promise an easy fix but offers something far more substantial: **a consistent method** for aligning your daily actions with your innermost values—a powerful strategy for living not just any life, but one you love deeply.

As we reach the end of this chapter on taking inspired action, let's reiterate the essence of moving from intention to tangible progress. By breaking down your goals, building momentum, and overcoming obstacles, you've equipped yourself with a robust framework to navigate the complexities of personal and professional growth. The strategies discussed here are designed to help you tackle the initial overwhelm that often accompanies new ambitions and guide you toward consistent, actionable steps forward.

Step-by-Step Process: "The Action Blueprint"

1. **Define Your Goals Clearly**: Start by writing down your long-term aspirations across various aspects of your life—career, personal development, relationships, and health. This clarity will serve as the foundation for all subsequent actions.

2. **Prioritize and Focus**: Evaluate your goals based on their urgency and relevance. Select one or two that resonate deeply with you and dedicate your initial efforts to these areas.

3. **Break Goals into Steps**: Deconstruct your chosen goals into manageable tasks. Set up SMART goals for each task to ensure they are specific, measurable, achievable, relevant, and time-bound. For example, if transitioning to a new career is your goal, begin by researching potential fields, updating your resume, and networking with industry professionals.

4. **Track Your Progress**: Implement a system to monitor your achievements and upcoming tasks—be it a digital tool or a simple planner. This will help you maintain a clear view of your progress and adjust your strategies as needed.

5. **Build a Support Network**: Share your goals with friends or connect with like-minded individuals who are also pursuing significant changes. This network will provide motivation and accountability.

6. **Prepare for Challenges**: Anticipate possible obstacles and think through solutions beforehand. Tools like visualization and affirmations can reinforce your resolve during tough times.

7. **Review and Adjust Regularly**: Set regular intervals to review what you've accomplished and what's ahead. Celebrate your successes, no matter how small, and refine your approach if certain strategies aren't working as expected.

8. **Allow Flexibility**: While it's important to have a structured plan, remain open to adjustments. Life's unpredictability requires a flexible approach to goal achievement.

This blueprint is not just about achieving specific goals but also about fostering personal growth and self-awareness through each step you take. Remember, the key is not just to dream, but to act with intention and insight.

By embracing these principles, you set the stage for meaningful change in your life. Each small step is a building block in constructing a resilient, fulfilling future where your actions align closely with your deepest values and aspirations. Let this chapter be a turning point where you shift from aspiration to actualization, using mindfulness to stay connected to your purpose and progress. Keep pushing boundaries, stay consistent, and remember that each step forward, no matter how small, is a crucial part of your bigger picture.

Chapter Ten

Leading with Your Heart

Can Small Goals Truly Change a Life?

Maria stood by her kitchen window, the early morning light casting a warm glow over the old wooden table where she usually had her coffee. She watched as the steam rose in soft spirals from her mug, the aroma of freshly brewed beans mingling with the scent of damp earth from the garden outside. Today felt different, like a small turning point in an otherwise cyclic existence.

She had been feeling aimless lately, her days blending into one another without distinction. The bookstore she managed was more than just a job; it was a sanctuary. Yet, even surrounded by stories of adventure and triumph, Maria felt anchored in place by her own uncertainties. The idea of setting small goals had come to her like a whisper among the stacks of books she lovingly cared for.

Her mind wandered to last night's conversation with an old friend who seemed to have found direction through setting such goals. *"It's about celebrating the little victories,"* he had said, his voice crackling through the phone line, *"like finishing a book or even just organizing your desk."*

The bell above the door jingled softly as Maria entered her bookstore later that morning. She ran her fingers across the spines of books as she walked through aisles lined with towering shelves. Each book was a world unto itself, and she wondered how many contained characters who felt just as lost as she did.

A young woman approached her hesitantly, holding a copy of "The Alchemist." *"I heard this is about finding one's destiny,"* she said quietly.

"Yes," Maria replied, feeling a kinship with both the customer and the protagonist of that novel. *"It's about discovering what is truly important to you."*

As the day unfolded with customers coming and going, Maria kept thinking about goals—small yet significant. Perhaps today's goal could be as simple as recommending books to at least five customers based on their stories rather than their queries alone.

Later, sitting in the quiet backroom surrounded by piles of unsorted books and notes for upcoming displays, Maria reflected on her day. Each recommendation she made felt like planting seeds in fertile ground—seeds that might someday grow into trees sturdy enough to stand on their own.

The room smelled faintly of paper and ink—a comforting scent that always soothed her nerves. She realized that these minor achievements were stepping stones; they were building blocks leading somewhere brighter and more confident.

As twilight approached and painted soft shadows on the floor of her shop, Maria locked up for the night. Walking home under a sky turning shades of pink and purple, she thought about tomorrow's goals. Maybe they would be slightly bigger than today's goals—perhaps organizing an author meet or setting up that display window she'd been planning for weeks.

How often do we overlook these small steps towards our larger dreams? Could it be that within these modest beginnings lie our greatest opportunities for growth?

Discovering the Power of Goal Setting: A Roadmap to Confidence and Clarity

In this pivotal chapter, we explore the transformative impact of goal setting on your confidence and life direction. Often, we find ourselves at a crossroads, overwhelmed by indecision and stifled by uncertainties. It's here, in these moments of doubt, that the strategy of setting clear, achievable goals becomes, not just useful, but essential. This approach serves as a compass, guiding you through the fog of daily life and aligning you with your true aspirations.

Recognizing Small Wins

The journey begins with embracing vulnerability. It's about acknowledging where you are now and setting sights on where you want to be. By defining small, attainable goals, you create opportunities for frequent achievements. These victories, no matter how minor they may seem, are pivotal. They bolster your self-esteem and reinforce the belief that larger successes are within reach.

Each goal achieved is a step out of invisibility and into a state of empowerment.

Envisioning Your Life with Purpose

Living with intention is more than just a catchphrase; it's a structured method for manifesting the life you desire. This chapter will show you how to paint a vivid picture of your ideal future. With every brushstroke shaped by intention, you'll learn to lay down the practical steps required to turn your vision into reality. This isn't about grandiose dreams but setting a course for achievable realities that resonate deeply with your personal values and desires.

Cultivating Lasting Happiness

Sustaining joy and connection comes from consistently applying what you've learned about yourself through intentional living. We'll discuss strategies for maintaining balance and joy in your life—ensuring that the authenticity you've worked so hard to cultivate doesn't fade over time, but grows stronger. This is about making happiness a habit, rooted deeply in everyday actions and decisions.

As we edge closer to the conclusion of this guide, it's crucial to reflect on how these elements interlink with the broader themes of the book—reclaiming your confidence, rediscovering your identity, and embracing a life unmarred by fear or guilt. Through practical examples and actionable advice, this chapter doesn't just sketch an outline for personal growth; it offers a detailed blueprint.

Building from Within

This chapter underscores the critical role that tailored goal setting plays in personal development. By starting small, recognizing your progress, and continuously aligning with your core values, you can effectively transform feelings of aimlessness into directions of purpose and clarity.

In essence, 'Leading with Your Heart' encapsulates the essence of breaking free from fear—each page crafted to guide you through rediscovering who you are meant to be without being overwhelmed by life's demands. Here lies not just advice but a call to action: prioritize yourself in a world that often tells women otherwise.

Through real-life success stories and simple yet profound insights into human psychology, this chapter offers both motivation and method. It invites you to step confidently towards crafting a narrative of success defined on your own terms—a narrative where fear has no stronghold and authenticity reigns supreme.

Embracing Vulnerability

Vulnerability is often seen as a weakness, but it is truly a strength. When we allow ourselves to be vulnerable, we open up to genuine connections and deeper understanding. It's about showing our true selves, not just to others, but to ourselves as well. This opening up can be frightening, indeed, but it is also a powerful step towards authenticity.

Imagine vulnerability as a window. Most of the time, we keep the curtains drawn, shielded from the outside view, safe but isolated. By pulling back the curtain, we let light flood in, revealing both our internal mess and beauty. This act doesn't just clarify our vision; it invites others to see us as we truly are, fostering deeper bonds and a genuine sense of belonging.

The facts support this: research shows that people who practice vulnerability are better able to build strong, lasting relationships. These relationships form the foundation of both personal and professional success. By embracing vulnerability, we not only enhance our connections with others but also boost our self-confidence, as we are no longer burdened by the weight of hiding our true selves.

However, vulnerability is not about over-sharing or seeking approval. It's a balanced approach where we share our feelings and experiences with those who have earned our trust. It's about being honest about our emotions and needs without fear of judgment. This kind of open communication is crucial for building trust and fostering an environment where everyone can feel safe to express themselves.

Embracing vulnerability allows us to connect more deeply with others and ourselves.

Living with Intention

Living with intention means making choices that align with our deepest values and aspirations. It's about steering our lives in a direction that leads to fulfillment and growth, rather than drifting along without purpose. This proactive approach to life empowers us to create the reality we envision and desire.

Setting intentional goals is like planting a garden. Just as a gardener selects seeds thoughtfully, plants them, and nurtures them to grow, we must choose our goals based on what we value and wish to achieve, then take consistent action to nurture these goals to fruition.

Knowing what we want, and why we want it is the first step in living intentionally. This clarity is crucial because it guides our decisions and actions. It's the difference between reacting to life and responding to it with a clear mind. When we know our 'why', every 'how' becomes more apparent, and our daily actions gain purpose.

Living intentionally also involves reflecting regularly on our progress and adjusting our paths as needed. Life is unpredictable, and flexibility is key to maintaining our course when unexpected challenges arise. This adaptability ensures that we remain aligned with our values and goals, even when circumstances change.

By living intentionally, we not only enhance our own lives but also positively impact those around us. Our actions and attitudes can inspire others to think about their own lives and make changes that lead to greater happiness and satisfaction.

How will recognizing and aligning your daily actions with your core values change your life?

Sustaining Joy and Connection

The Joyful Living Framework is a system designed to help individuals maintain the joy and authenticity they've worked hard to cultivate. It consists of three interconnected components: Vulnerability Acceptance, Intentional Visioning, and Joyful Literacy. Each plays a crucial role in creating a fulfilling life narrative.

Vulnerability Acceptance

Vulnerability Acceptance is about seeing vulnerability as a strength rather than a weakness. This component encourages sharing personal stories and emotions with trusted individuals, thereby fostering deeper connections and authenticity. It's about being open and real, which, in turn, enhances our relationships and our self-esteem.

Intentional Visioning

Intentional Visioning involves crafting a clear and detailed vision of one's ideal life, emphasizing the importance of daily actions that align with long-term aspirations. This vision acts as a compass, guiding individuals through the complexities of life while keeping them connected to their core values. Tools like vision boards and journaling are suggested to help maintain focus and track progress.

Joyful Literacy

Joyful Literacy teaches the art of recognizing and cultivating moments of joy in everyday life. It promotes mindfulness and gratitude, essential practices for sustaining happiness. By appreciating the small joys, individuals can maintain a positive outlook and a resilient spirit, even during challenging times.

The dynamics of the Joyful Living Framework involve the continuous interplay between these components. As individuals practice vulnerability, they become more authentic, which enhances their relationships. This authenticity makes their visioning more meaningful and aligned, which in turn, makes it easier to recognize joy in the small moments. Over time, this creates a reinforcing loop of positivity and growth.

By integrating these three components... Vulnerability Acceptance, Intentional Visioning,

and Joyful Literacy... we can sustain the joy and connection we've cultivated, thus leading a truly fulfilling life.

As we draw this guide to a close, it's vital to reflect on how the principles of embracing vulnerability, living with intention, and sustaining joy and connection can significantly reshape your life. These concepts are not just theoretical but are practical and actionable strategies that have the power to transform your daily experiences and overall well-being.

Embracing vulnerability is your first step toward genuine self-discovery. By allowing yourself to be open and authentic, you set the stage for deeper connections with others and a more fulfilling life. It's about acknowledging that strength truly comes from facing your fears and opening up about your challenges.

Living with intention moves you from a passive state to an active one where you are in control of shaping your future. This involves setting clear, attainable goals which not only motivate but also guide you towards your larger aspirations. It's about making conscious choices every day that align with your core values and long-term vision.

Finally, **sustaining joy and connection** ensures that the progress you make is lasting. It's crucial to find balance and maintain the changes you've worked so hard to implement. This means regularly revisiting your goals, adapting them as needed, and continuing to engage with supportive communities that reinforce your new way of living.

Throughout this book, we've tackled the significant challenge of reconnecting with your True-Self and shedding the weight of external expectations. The strategies discussed here are designed to help you build a life where self-care becomes a priority without the accompanying guilt. This shift not only enhances your confidence, but also empowers you to live authentically.

By applying these principles, you'll notice a profound change in how you view yourself and how you interact with the world around you. Remember, the path to a life filled with purpose and joy is ongoing and ever-evolving. Keep striving towards your goals with the confidence that you are fully capable of achieving them.

Let this be the moment you choose to act. Take the insights and tools provided and start making changes today. Your authentic life awaits, and it's more attainable than you might think. Embrace it with open arms and an open heart.

Chapter Eleven

Conclusion

A Radiant, Bold You

Reflecting on the Journey

Take a moment to think back to the version of yourself who started this book. Close your eyes if you need to. Picture her—her worries, her doubts, her frustrations. What was she longing for? What was holding her back? What did she believe about herself that wasn't serving her?

Now, think about who you are today.

You've read the pages of this book and, more importantly, you've engaged with them. Maybe you've journaled through the exercises, taken small steps to set boundaries, or even found yourself standing a little taller in conversations that used to make you feel small.

Whether you've made monumental changes or taken the tiniest steps, you've done something incredible—you've shown up for yourself. And that deserves to be celebrated.

There's a reason why so many people stay stuck: change is uncomfortable. It requires us to examine our fears, rewrite our narratives, and move forward without guarantees. But you did it anyway. You decided that your well-being, your confidence, and your happiness were worth it.

That's not just courage—it's power.

And while this book may be coming to an end, your journey isn't. In fact, it's only just beginning. What you've started here is a process of uncovering who you are and reclaiming the life that has always been waiting for you. You've laid a foundation for growth, self-awareness, and resilience that will carry you forward in ways you may not even realize yet.

The Power of Small, Consistent Steps

One of the most important lessons I hope you take from this book is this: meaningful change doesn't happen overnight. It doesn't require massive, sweeping gestures or a complete overhaul of your life. It happens through the small, deliberate steps you take each day.

Consider the ways you've already started to build momentum. Maybe you've begun setting boundaries with loved ones, or you've started carving out a few minutes of quiet time just for yourself. Maybe you've stopped apologizing unnecessarily, or you've allowed yourself to dream again—bold, beautiful dreams that light you up inside.

Every one of those steps matters.

Real growth comes from consistency, not perfection. You don't have to have it all figured out or get everything *"right"* to see progress. The woman you are becoming isn't the result of one grand decision; she's the result of all the little choices you make to prioritize yourself, trust yourself, and believe in yourself.

And remember, you're allowed to stumble. Progress is rarely linear, and setbacks are part of the process. What matters is that you keep going. When fear or doubt creeps in, remind yourself of how far you've already come. Let that be your fuel to keep moving forward.

Living Boldly and Without Apology

Let's talk about what it means to live boldly.

It doesn't mean you have to be fearless—fear is natural, and sometimes it even protects us. Living boldly means acknowledging the fear and choosing to move forward anyway. It means allowing yourself to take up space, speak your truth, and pursue the things that make your heart come alive.

Bold living looks different for everyone. For some, it might mean starting a new career, traveling to a place they've always dreamed of, or tackling a big, audacious goal. For others, it might be as simple as saying no to something they don't want to do, sharing their opinion in a meeting, or looking in the mirror and smiling at the person they see.

What does living boldly look like for you?

You don't need permission to live this way, and you certainly don't need to justify it to anyone else. Boldness is about authenticity—it's about aligning your actions with your values and choosing a life that feels true to you.

Living unapologetically doesn't mean you'll never face criticism or doubt. It means those things will no longer control you. When you embrace your truth, you'll find a strength you never knew you had.

Sustaining Your Growth

As you move forward, remember that the tools you've learned here are meant to grow with you. The confidence you've begun to reclaim, the boundaries you've set, the goals you've started pursuing—all of these are part of an ongoing process.

You will continue to evolve, and that's something to celebrate. As your life changes, your needs and priorities will, too. Stay connected to yourself. Make space to reflect, adjust, and recalibrate as needed. Trust that you have the wisdom to navigate whatever comes next.

And don't forget to surround yourself with people who uplift and inspire you. Growth isn't meant to happen in isolation. Find your community—whether it's close friends, a mentor, or a group of like-minded women who understand what it means to grow and thrive.

A Final Word

Thank you for letting me be part of your journey. Writing this book wasn't just about sharing strategies; it was about offering a hand to women like you who are ready to step out of the shadows and into the light.

You are not invisible. You are not alone. You never were. You've always had the power to show up boldly, speak your truth, and create a life that feels deeply fulfilling. This book didn't give you that power—it's been in you all along. What it did was remind you of what you're capable of.

So as you close these pages and move forward, hold on to this truth: You are worthy. You are enough. You are capable of doing hard things and of living a life that is unapologetically yours.

The courage to be you isn't something you find—it's something you choose.

Now, go live it.

With gratitude and belief in you,

Chrissy Shaver

Chapter Twelve

Epilogue

Stepping Forward with Confidence and Authenticity

As we draw to a close, let's reflect on the insights we've shared and consider how they can be woven into the fabric of your daily life. The principles outlined in these pages are more than just concepts; they are practical tools designed to help you reclaim your sense of Self and not to mention the Badassery of your own Heart to live life like you want it.

Bringing the Book to Life: Practical Applications

Imagine applying the strategies discussed here in your everyday interactions and decisions. Whether it's setting boundaries, practicing self-care, or making time for your passions, these actions foster a deeper connection with your authentic Self. By consistently applying these principles, you not only enhance your own life, but also set a powerful example for those around you.

Recap of Core Ideas

We began by addressing the common feelings of invisibility and disconnection from oneself, which many women experience due to incessant demands on their time and energy. We explored how to identify and dismantle the fears that prevent personal growth and discussed strategies for building a robust sense of self-worth. Remember, recognizing your needs does not diminish your ability to care for others; it enhances it.

Guidance for Implementation

To integrate these ideas into your life:

- **Start small**: Choose one area where you feel you can make an immediate change.
- **Be consistent**: Implementing small changes consistently leads to significant long-term benefits.

- **Seek support**: Share your goals with trusted friends or family members who can provide encouragement.

Acknowledging Limitations

While the strategies provided are crafted with care, individual experiences may vary. Personal growth is a complex, deeply personal endeavor that might require tailored approaches not fully covered in this book. I encourage you to seek additional resources or professional guidance if you find yourself needing more specialized support.

Call to Action

I urge you to take the first step today. Choose one strategy from this book that resonates with you and commit to trying it out this week. Each small step is a building block towards a more fulfilled and authentic life.

A Lasting Impression

In closing, remember that true change comes from within. It isn't always easy or straightforward, but it is always worth it. Hold on to the vision of the life you aspire to—not just for yourself, but as a beacon for those you love.

"The only limit to our realization of tomorrow will be our doubts of today." **— Franklin D. Roosevelt**

Let this quote remind you that your current limitations or fears are merely stepping stones on the path to a brighter, more authentic existence.

Chapter Thirteen

Your Next Step...

Here's How To Unlock Your Confidence, Reclaim Your Identity, and Thrive Authentically in Just Months—Despite Life's Overwhelming Demands...

WE'VE REACHED THE END of our time together, my friend. I sincerely hope that you've benefited from reading my book in more ways than one.

The next step for you is simple:

Get started!

Taking action is your immediate step. Nothing happens until you make it happen. You now have everything you need to add health and fitness into your life.

Still not sure of where to start, or exactly what to do?

I'm more than happy to help you get everything in place, and achieve that empowered and joyful life you deserve.

If you'd like me to help, reach out to me by scheduling a **https://tinyurl.com/chrissy-shaver**. If you enjoyed this book, you'll do even better with me leading the way.

Instead of trying to figure everything out yourself, I'm happy to help you by clarifying anything you read in this book that you're not quite sure about, or even want more details specific to your current situation and **how to live your life boldly and without apology**. No risk, no obligation. Just me helping you determine the best plan of action. I help busy adults just like you take charge of their lives, both personally and professionally. And they stick to it.

Step 1: We spend time together outlining and developing your habits, dreams, life goals, and overall strategies to fully create the perfect solution for you.

Step 2: We begin integrating your new strategies and habits into your busy schedule.

Step 3: We dial everything into your current lifestyle to make adding empowering habits align with your busy life. Together we make it a walk in the park.

Step 4: Once we have your habits and strategies down pat, we monitor everything to ensure everything is working seamlessly to get you the greatest results in the shortest time.

Most busy adults think they are prisoners of their current situation, and living an empowered and joyful life is not within their reach.

Truth is, my done-with-you program is designed to make it an easy and stress-free transition for you, so we give you everything you need to ensure your success in the shortest possible time.

If you're ready to add empowerment and joyful happiness into your life that gets twice the results in half the time, let's get on a **https://tinyurl.com/chrissy-shaver**.

About the Author

Who is Chrissy Shaver?

Reclaiming Confidence, Identity, and Badass Self-Care

For many women, life becomes a delicate balancing act—juggling responsibilities, caring for loved ones, and pushing personal needs to the bottom of the list. Chrissy Shaver knows this all too well. A heart-centered transformational fitness professional, Chrissy dedicates her work to helping women, ages 25-65, who have lost their sense of Self and confidence. Her mission is simple yet profound: to empower women to step out of the shadows, find strength in their voice, reconnect with their hearts, and embrace the vibrant, unapologetic life they've always imagined.

Chrissy's journey into fitness coaching isn't just about movement—it's about transformation. She understands that fitness is more than exercise; it's a powerful tool for personal growth, confidence-building, and identity reclamation. For the women Chrissy serves, it's not about fitting into a mold but about breaking free from one. Through a combination of strength coaching, holistic self-care strategies, and heart-centered empowerment, Chrissy guides her clients on a journey to rediscover the badass versions of themselves that have been quietly waiting for permission to shine.

Understanding the Pain: A Coach Who Truly Sees You

Chrissy's clients often share similar struggles. They feel invisible, stuck in a cycle of daydreaming about the life they want but unable to take action. They've spent years prioritizing others, from raising children to supporting partners or thriving in demanding careers, often at the expense of their own needs. Many of them harbor fears of being judged or failing, leaving them paralyzed by self-doubt.

Chrissy sees these women—their potential, their resilience, and the spark that's still burning deep within. She knows they're not broken; they're simply disconnected from their true selves. Chrissy provides a safe and supportive space for her clients to explore what they want out of life, free from guilt or shame. Her coaching is not about forcing change, but about guiding her clients to unlock their inner strength and discover their confidence.

The Solution: Movement, Voice, and Heart

Chrissy's approach is as unique as the women she serves. She uses fitness as a foundation to build physical strength and emotional resilience, proving that movement is a gateway to transformation. But her coaching doesn't stop at exercise. Chrissy's programs blend physical activity with mindset work, encouraging her clients to use their voices and lead with their hearts.

She works closely with her clients to create customized badass self-care routines that are practical, sustainable, and deeply personal. Chrissy understands that self-care isn't selfish—it's essential. Through this process, her clients learn to prioritize themselves without feeling guilty, discovering that they can serve others more effectively by first taking care of their own needs.

Empowered Women, Empowered Lives

The results Chrissy delivers are life-changing. Her clients not only see physical improvements—such as increased strength, better posture, and higher energy—but they also experience profound emotional and mental shifts. They begin to live life on their own terms, no longer hiding from opportunities or fearing judgment. Chrissy's coaching instills a sense of pride, self-love, and boldness, empowering her clients to pursue their dreams and make their voices heard.

One of Chrissy's core beliefs is that every woman has the right to live fully and authentically. She challenges societal norms that tell women to shrink, to be quiet, or to stay in the background. Instead, Chrissy equips her clients with the tools and confidence to step into the spotlight and take up the space they deserve.

Inspiration for the Reader: Your Transformation Awaits

Chrissy Shaver's work is more than fitness—it's a movement. It's an invitation to reclaim your life, rewrite your story, and rediscover the badass version of yourself that's been patiently waiting for the chance to shine. Whether you're 25 or 65, whether you've been hiding from the mirror or dreaming of a new chapter, Chrissy is here to remind you that it's never too late to take control of your life.

With her support, you'll learn to embrace movement, use your voice, and lead with your heart. You'll stop daydreaming and start living. Chrissy's coaching will show you that prioritizing yourself isn't selfish—it's the key to unlocking the confident, joyful, and empowered life you've always deserved.

Are you ready to be seen, heard, and celebrated? Let Chrissy Shaver guide you on the journey to reclaiming your badass Self. Because the best version of you is just waiting to be unleashed.

Made in the USA
Middletown, DE
13 February 2025